The Way of Individuation

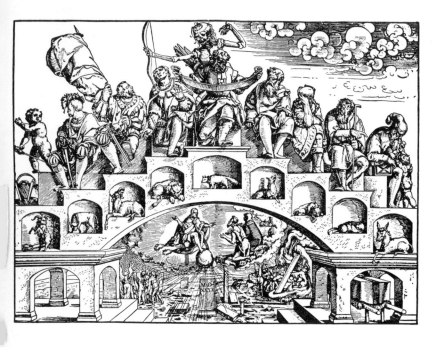

Engraving by Jörg Breu d. J., ca. 1530, in which the ten stages of life are represented by human figures of corresponding age, each being associated with an animal: the infant with a goat, the boy with a calf, the youth with a horse, the man of forty with a lion, of fifty with a fox, of sixty with a dog, of seventy with an ox, of eighty with a bear, of ninety with a donkey, but the man of one hundred with a coffin. These attributes are meant to characterize the qualities of the respective ages. The figures are arranged in a semi-circle; at the top stands Death, symbol of the transcience of earthly existence. The lower semi-circle depicts the Last Judgment.

Jolande Jacobi

THE WAY OF
INDIVIDUATION

Translated by R. F. C. Hull

A Helen and Kurt Wolff Book
Harcourt, Brace & World, Inc., New York

This book is dedicated to my grandson Christian,
for his life's journey

PREFACE

In a letter to me dated 24 September 1948 Jung wrote: "The systematic elaboration of my ideas, which were often just thrown out, is a task for those who come after me, and unless it is accomplished there will be no progress in the science of analytical psychology." This statement was a challenge I have tried to meet, to the best of my knowledge and ability, with this little book as a modest contribution to Jung's expectations. It is the product of many years of reflection and observation, of careful study, of quiet hours of meditation and, not least, of personal and practical experience. The way of individuation as the keystone of Jung's widely ramifying work is particularly suited to signalize the position which distinguishes it from other schools of psychology. It amounts to a comprehensive view of life which embraces the all-too-human as well as the personal and the suprapersonal. Individuation, understood as the growing self-awareness of the individual and society, and expressed also in the transformation of man's idea of God in correspondence with the ruling state of consciousness, is a social, ethical, and religious problem which is more important for us than ever today if we are not only to endure the present but also shape a better future. Yet, precisely because Jung's concept of individuation is so interwoven with the many-sidedness of human existence, it has often been misunderstood or, more often, not understood at all. The methodical clarification of this centrepiece of Jungian psychology, which is of the greatest significance not only in psychotherapy but also as the goal of human development in general, therefore seemed urgently called for. It was a task I had much at heart, moreover, as the confession of a life rich in experience. Much of the joy and sorrow of a long life was built into it and applied to the supplementing and rounding out of Jung's ideas.

If, nevertheless, certain things could not be brought into clear enough focus, and others have still remained dark to logical, rational thinking, I would, by way of exonerating myself, quote Jung's own words, in which he points out the difficulties of presenting such a theme. In his memoirs he says: "The reality of life, with all its abysses and terrors, its unpredictable qualities, cannot be covered by so-called 'clear concepts.'" And again: "I strive quite consciously and deliberately for ambiguity of expression, because it is superior to singleness of meaning and reflects the nature of life. My whole temperament inclines me to be very unequivocal indeed. That is not difficult, but it would be at the cost of truth." At the same time he emphasized that he "took great care to try to understand every single image, every item of my psychic inventory, and to classify them scientifically—so far as this was possible."

As a creative person, as an artist, one might say, Jung was conditioned through and through by spiritual forces and open to their influences. But as a man of science, to whose requirements he felt the deepest obligations, all his efforts were directed towards systematizing his experiences and ideas and expressing them in the clearest possible concepts. The present book could not ignore this dual nature of Jung's work, and it must therefore appeal to the goodwill not only of those who devote themselves to understanding both these realms, but also to the devotees of the rational and of the irrational.

In the preparation of the book I am indebted for much help to the editor and faithful recorder of Jung's memoirs, Frau Aniela Jaffé. Dr. Josef Rudin read the text, with particular attention to the religious aspects. Dr. Ernst Spengler and my son Andrew gave helpful support in correcting the manuscript and the proofs. To all I would like to express my warmest thanks.

Thus, not without inward emotion, and mindful of the necessary inadequacy of my work, I set forth on this exacting theme: *habent sua fata libelli.* Let it fare as fate wills.

JOLANDE JACOBI

Zurich, summer 1965

CONTENTS

The Way of Individuation

The Forerunners

Tʀᴜᴇ scientific knowledge does not consist only in answering the question of the What. It reaches fulfilment only when it is able to discover the Whence and to combine it with the Whither. Knowing becomes understanding only when it embraces the beginning, the continuation, and the end."

These words of J. J. Bachofen (1815–1887), C. G. Jung's great countryman, taken from the introduction to his book *Mutterrecht* (1861), might serve as a motto for that unitary, teleological view of the psyche from which is also derived Jung's concept of the "individuation process". They anticipate by some eighty years an attitude which, after the atomistic, mechanistic views of the late nineteenth century had been superseded, moulded the vision of the homogeneity of all psychic events. Basic to this attitude was the idea that psychic life should be regarded as a meaningfully ordered process containing its goal within itself. Ever since the broad sweep of the Romantic view of the world, with its feeling for the unity of life, this vision has never quite been lost. We meet it already in C. G. Carus (1789–1869), in whose work we find many features that have an affinity with Jung's ideas. Thus R. Marx writes in the introduction to Carus' *Psyche* (1846): "Indeed, looking at life more closely, we see that in its continuous striving there must remain present a feeling, an unconscious memory of what

3

was present before, otherwise it would be inexplicable how, at the peak of development, after passing through many phases, something can come back again formed in exactly the same way as the germ from which the development started (e.g., the egg or the seed); and again, we perceive that there must dwell within it a definite, even though unconscious foreknowledge of whither its course of development is tending and what it is seeking, otherwise the sure progress, the regular preparation of numerous phenomena that in themselves can only be transitional phases, and that subordinate themselves to ever higher aims, would be wholly inexplicable." [1] In these sentences we cannot but hear a spiritual note struck which also echoes in Jung's writings.

With the endeavours to understand personal development as a goal-directed unfolding and organization of innate tendencies and dispositions, there arose in the nineteenth century a number of psychological theories which treated the subject in all sorts of variations; there were, for instance, a deterministic, a vitalistic, a personalistic, a developmental, a genetic, a Gestalt psychology, among others. They are associated primarily with the names of W. Wundt, F. Krüger, K. Koffka, W. Stern, Charlotte and K. Bühler, E. Spranger, and many more besides. It would, however, be wrong to regard the view which sees life as a unity, even though with various sub-divisions, as an invention of scientific psychology.

Human life considered as a homogeneous process, as a development in "stages" each with its own peculiarities and distinguishing marks, is an age-old view which crops up again and again in the literature of the West. There are, as the case may be, two, three, four, and even ten segments or stages into which our life is divided from the cradle to the grave.

The simplest form, division into two, consists only of youth and age. The division into three follows the course of the sun: morning, noon, evening, their parallels being youth, manhood, age, as portrayed for instance in the pictures of the three Magi: Caspar is the youth, Balthazar the man, Melchior the grey-

beard.² The famous picture of "Prudentia", attributed to Titian, represents the same situation, but here the three human
heads are correlated with three animals—wolf, lion, dog.³ The
division into four is based on the four seasons. It corresponds
to the ancient Roman sequence: *puer, juvenis, vir, senex.* To
these is added, in the division into five, *virilitas,* dignified maturity, or, as in Varro, *infantia.* In the fivefold division the
stages last fourteen years; they therefore go in cycles of twice
seven. The commonest sub-divisions are into seven or ten
stages. The former are correlated with the planets, it being
said that the first ten years come under the influence of Mer-
cury, the second ten under that of Venus, the third under that
of Mars, etc., the last ten under that of Saturn.⁴ After seventy
one would come under the influence of Uranus.

Here we may quote an amusing folk-poem which says:

> A fence lasts three years,
> A dog outlives three fences,
> A horse outlives three dogs,
> A man outlives three horses,
> A donkey outlives three men,
> A wild goose outlives three donkeys,
> A crow outlives three wild geese,
> A stag outlives three crows,
> A raven outlives three stags.
> Thus to man are allotted 81 years,
> But to the phoenix 177,147.

"The years of our life are threescore and ten, and even by
reason of strength fourscore," says the Psalmist.⁵ In the ten-
stage sequence, life goes on till a hundred and witnesses to
man's unfading hope for the longest possible existence on
earth.⁶ Another folk-poem says:

> He who in twenty years does not get thin,
> And in thirty years does not get sick,
> And in thirty-five does not get strong,
> And in forty does not get mean,
> And in forty-five does not get brave,

And in sixty-five does not get rich,
And in seventy-five does not get wise,
And in eighty-five does not go gray,
And in ninety-five does not get caught,
And in a hundred does not get hanged,
And should outlive all this span,
God! He's been a lucky man.

Man's fate unfolds itself stage by stage, like a bud that harbours within it a blossom. The idea of these stages has penetrated deep into the soul of the people, leaving its deposit in countless documents of folk-literature and often also in poetry and the arts. It has given rise to an infinity of sayings, stories, pictures, all fraught with symbols. The following Oriental fairytale is a delightful example:

"The Lord God, wishing to fix the life-span of his creatures, gave the donkey, the dog, and the ape, and finally also man, thirty years apiece. But that was too much for the animals, and God took pity on them and gave the donkey only eighteen years, the dog only twelve, and the ape only ten. But for man thirty years was too little, and God took pity on him and gave him in addition the eighteen, twelve, and ten years of the animals. That is why, for his first thirty years, man lives a human life; then, one after another, he is overtaken by the burdensome years of the donkey, the snarling years of the dog, and the foolish years of the ape, a thing for children to laugh at. The thirty human years are followed by forty animal years, and thus man has seventy years to live." [7]

Life as the wheel of fortune, the spokes symbolizing its individual phases, or as a tree with widely ramifying branches—these are ever recurrent images. Often it is described as a "journey" or a "wandering", or as La Rochefoucauld says: "Our life is like a jaunt in the mountains with unexpected views, turns in the way, resting-places, and a goal we do not know." [8] Being an optimist, he does not mention the dangers and the abysses. Plausible and apt as these images are, they remain in the realm of the biological and the everyday and do not shed light on the deeper meaning of life's course.

With the steady mounting of man's life-expectancy during the last century and, as a result, the unusual increase in the number of old people, the problem has shifted its ground in a fundamental way. It is evident that a completely new relation to the course of life has to be found, above all to the problem of growing old, which must be accorded a new value. If the ancient Romans called the first thirty years of life *aetas*, i.e., a generation, this meant that the reproductive capacity and the family, or the biological and social task, occupied the foreground. But when there is an average life-expectancy of seventy years, the spiritual and psychic task also makes its demands if man is to win a satisfying meaning for his life and to find its destination.

Charlotte Bühler deserves credit for her scientific attempts to investigate the problems connected with the course of human life viewed as a unity. From a careful evaluation of answers to questionnaires and from a mass of biographical data she describes in her book[9] a series of typical life-courses, or life-structures, which display a certain regularity. Her conclusion that man's creative task, the specifically human criterion of a fully valid existence, is "to be there for something, whether this be a human being, a thing, a work, an idea,"[10] hits the mark. She proposes a biological ground-plan (*A*) of the course of life, supplementing it with a spiritual-psychic ground-plan (dotted line) whose course, depending on the individual's own efforts, his gifts and his fate, can take a different direction from the biological. This line of development can surpass and transcend it, meeting it again only at the moment of death.

Within the biological ground-plan Charlotte Bühler distinguishes two main directions: the period of expansion up to about the forty-fifth year, and the period of restriction from then till the end of life. The life-course is divided into three main phases: from birth to the twenty-fifth year (phase I), from the twenty-fifth to the forty-fifth (phase III), from the forty-fifth to the seventieth (phase V), and into two transitional phases, in which the change of direction and the alternation of generations occur: from the fifteenth to the twenty-fifth year

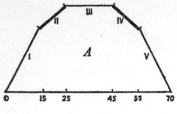

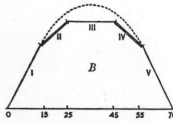

A. *The biological ground-plan.*

B. *The "normal structure" for the course of spiritual life. Here the spiritual culmination coincides with the biological, in phase III, rising and falling equally rapidly.*

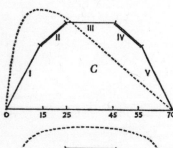

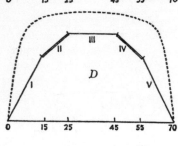

C. *Here the spiritual culmination occurs already in phase II, the first transitional phase.*

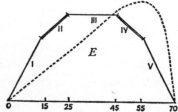

D. *Here an early culmination continues until the end of life.*

E. *Here the culmination occurs only in phase IV, the second transitional phase, and lasts till death.*

(phase II), and from the forty-fifth to the fiftieth or sixtieth (phase IV). In the first transitional phase reproductive capacity sets in, in the second it ceases. In the so-called "normal structure" (B) the spiritual-psychic culmination coincides with the biological: it occurs in the third, middle phase, between the twenty-fifth and the forty-fifth year.[11] In special cases the culmination can be reached earlier, as early as in phase II (C), and then suddenly sink or, more rarely, last a very long time, right up to phase V (D). But it can also occur rather late, in the middle of phase IV, and then last till death (E). The diagrams on page 8 may serve as illustrations.

A represents a life based wholly on the vital, D a life based wholly on the spiritual.[12] It is obvious that compared with the biological ground-plan the course of spiritual life can be either premature or retarded and can lead to a culmination in relatively early years (C) or in late age (E). In spiritual life the possibility of growth ceases only at death. In sum, Charlotte Bühler was able to show that there are typical differences in the life-course as well as differences in the time and duration of its culmination, and that a meaningful existence is possible whether life be short or long.

With these theses Charlotte Bühler took an important step in the direction of a unitary view. It comes close to Jung's own. Nevertheless her researches, despite her genuine attempt to penetrate more deeply, still remain exclusively based on a psychology of consciousness and its specific methods.

Alfred Adler, at one time a pupil of Freud's, likewise spoke in his individual psychology of a "guiding fiction" which stamps the whole life of man with a finalistic striving and is meant to satisfy his demand for an entrenched power position. "Power" in Adler's view is the aim that guides all human desires and actions, and to it is subordinated, consciously or unconsciously, everything a man does and feels. One cannot deny this view a certain justification, yet it is too one-sided and allows only a fragmentary grasp of human existence. It oversimplifies by reducing it to a single instinct or drive.

Hence it was reserved for depth psychology,[13] the new science that arose at the turn of the century, to paint a completely different picture of man and to investigate the psyche, in its totality and unity, empirically. This picture not only embraced the contents and processes of the conscious mind, but also took into account those which are to be found in the limitless realms of the unconscious psyche. This meant a revolutionary change in our understanding and assessment of psychic modes of behaviour, since the recognition was forced upon man that, besides his voluntary and knowing actions, there also exist in him impulses of which he is not the master and over which he has no power. It can readily be understood that depth psychology was, and often still is, hard put to it to make any headway.

With the rise and development of depth psychology the genetic-analytical viewpoint of Freud, and the teleological-synthetic viewpoint of Jung—both attained on the basis of bold pioneer work—acquired a special significance. It is true that Freud's view was directed exclusively to the "fate of the libido", of "sexual energy", on which, he maintained, sickness and health, indeed the whole life of man, depended and by which it was formed. He traced success or failure in the life of an individual to its instinctual basis and to the state of its development. He overlooked the paramount importance and independent role of spiritual, creative impulses and needs whose fulfilment is not tied to any particular age. These and the whole course of life were in his view determined—one might almost say predetermined—by the impressions and experiences of childhood. Thus later life became as it were an epiphenomenon of childhood events, having no genuine task of its own. Jung, on the other hand, directed his attention to the whole of human existence as such, from its beginning to its end, and endeavoured to reveal from within its aspect as a totality. We can trace in him the ideas of a meaningful, hidden "life-plan" with its "phases", which, as we saw, had always been present in the germ in folk-wisdom and had also been taken up in part by scientific psychology, but were now illuminated from a new vantage-point and put in a new context. The results of Charlotte Bühler's investigations of the life-course as a psychological problem point in the same direction, though she did not, like Jung, follow up the ways and means of inner development and try to realize them systematically in practice.

If one wishes to make clear Jung's position and to hear his answers to the questions raised by these problems, this can best be done by giving an account of what he has termed the "individuation process" and of its phenomenology. The nature, content, laws, and manifestations of this process, which he gained by years of careful observation and worked out by systematic comparative researches, constitute the pillars of his teaching, and the conclusions that may be drawn from them are highly characteristic of his position as a whole.

Individuation

THE term "individuation process" occurs for the first time in Jung's book *Psychological Types* (originally published 1921), but the idea of it can be found in his doctoral dissertation "On the Psychology and Pathology of So-called Occult Phenomena" (1902). It was a guiding idea that was to hold him in its grip all his life, and reached its culmination in his last major work, *Mysterium Coniunctionis* (1955–56). In that early dissertation he concluded, from his observations of a medium, that the "spirits" which manifested themselves during the séances represented an invasion of autonomous "splinter personalities" into the medium's field of consciousness, components of a more comprehensive personality hidden in the unconscious psyche. He says: "It is, therefore, conceivable that the phenomena of double consciousness are simply new character formations, or *attempts of the future personality to break through,* and that in consequence of special difficulties . . . they get bound up with peculiar disturbances of consciousness" (i.e., somnambulistic phenomena).[1] Therefore it remained Jung's untiring scientific and psychotherapeutic endeavour to work out a methodological procedure for bringing these components to consciousness and associating them with the ego, in order to realize the "greater personality" which is potentially present in every individual.

To describe in any detail Jung's widely ramifying work, which runs to some two hundred major and minor writings, would far exceed the scope of this book. But as the individuation process is the core of his teachings, containing many of his most essential discoveries and views, it may do duty for the rest. Further expositions must be left to other, more detailed studies of this field of work, which is far from having been thoroughly explored.

In scientific usage, the *principium individuationis* is defined as that principle on which depends the breaking up of the general into the particular, into single beings or individuals. It is "the *raison d'être* of individuals or particulars".[2] It is found in Aristotle, Albertus Magnus, Thomas Aquinas, Leibniz, Spinoza, Locke, and Schopenhauer—to name only a few great thinkers—and has been the passionate concern of many brilliant minds, prompting them to a wide variety of explanations and correlations.[3] In so far as the human individual may be regarded as a unique and indivisible whole, he embodies in its highest form the power inherent in that principle. At the same time, the *principium individuationis* can manifest itself in full force only when the building up of the personality it unconsciously anticipates is undertaken by the conscious ego.

So when Jung speaks of an individuation process that characterizes a possibility of development immanent in everyone and that culminates in rounding out the individual into a psychic whole,[4] his conception, though following the same line as the other philosophical definitions, is both broader and deeper, since it takes account not only of the conscious but also of the unconscious components of the psyche in their delicately balanced and creative interaction with the conscious mind. The beginning and end of psychic life are in his view inseparable, bound together at every moment in the thousand-branched stream of psychic energy which pours without cessation through all the reaches of the psyche.

In this psyche the energy is kept in a state of constant dynamic mobility by a subtle mechanism of self-regulation and

compensation, balanced between tension and stagnation. Birth
and death are only two poles of a homogeneous chain of being
whose individual links—the days and years of life—rise out of
the mists of fate and become visible in the foreground. These
links are from the beginning determined by a common meaning, which strives ceaselessly and autonomously for realization,
no matter whether they belong to the dark, unconscious side,
the shadowland of the past or future, or to the daylight of the
conscious present. The meaning manifests itself as the maturation process of the psyche and has as its aim the completion of
the personality through the maximal extension of its field of
consciousness. This presupposes the gradual integration *of unconscious contents that are capable of becoming conscious.*[5]
The psyche is the theatre of all our struggles for development.
It is the organ of experience pure and simple. The affirmation
of these struggles is "life"; negation of them means isolation,
resignation, desiccation.

The Two Kinds of Individuation

Fundamentally, individuation is a natural process immanent in every living organism. It can even be observed in inorganic matter, albeit only in basic outline. In crystals, for instance, something initially unformed moulds itself into a definite form in accordance with some hidden ground-plan.

The individuation process can either take place unconsciously, or it can be made conscious in various ways and brought to a high degree of differentiation. It goes without saying that there are any number of intermediate stages. Two main forms may be distinguished:

1. The natural process, occurring more or less autonomously and without the participation of consciousness, and

2. The "artificial" process, aided for instance by analysis, developed by definite methods, and consciously experienced.

In both forms the same power is at work, striving for maturation and self-realization from the seed to the fruit, to the invisible goal immanent within them. But the two forms are as different as, say, a wild fruit and a highly cultivated one. In the first case everything is left to the natural process; in the second, this is assisted, intensified, and consciously realized by the application of a specific technique.

Everything that lives matures; human beings mature, machines do not. Thus the natural process is goal-directed dyna-

mism, a way of development to which all life is subject. To this
form belong most of the psychologies that seek to understand
human life as a homogeneous process, likewise the theories of
Charlotte Bühler. "The urge and compulsion to self-realization [i.e., individuation] is a law of nature and thus of invin-
cible power, even though its effect, at the start, is insignificant
and improbable," [1] says Jung.

Like a seed growing into a tree, life unfolds stage by stage.
Triumphant ascent, collapse, crises, failures, and new beginnings strew the way. It is the path trodden by the great majority of mankind, as a rule unreflectingly, unconsciously, unsus-
pectingly, following its labyrinthine windings from birth to
death in hope and longing. It is hedged about with struggle
and suffering, joy and sorrow, guilt and error, and nowhere
is there security from catastrophe. For as soon as a man tries
to escape every risk and prefers to experience life only in his
head, in the form of ideas and fantasies, as soon as he surren-
ders to opinions of "how it ought to be" and, in order not to
make a false step, imitates others whenever possible, he forfeits
the chance of his own independent development. Only if he
treads the path bravely and flings himself into life, fearing no
struggle and no exertion and fighting shy of no experience,
will he mature his personality more fully than the man who is
ever trying to keep to the safe side of the road. As Schopenhauer says: "The first forty years of life furnish the text, while
the remaining thirty supply the commentary; without the commentary we are unable to understand aright the true sense and
coherence of the text, together with the moral it contains." [2]

The more biological a life is, particularly in its second half,
the more it can be said to "come to an end", and the more
powerfully those late years are shaped by the spirit, the more it
can be said to "come to completion". Generally speaking, there
is a polar relationship between the two forms of life, since the
one often develops at the expense of the other. We observe, for
instance, that spiritually strong, creative people, the so-called
"geniuses", are often weak biologically and compensate this
weakness by their outstanding spiritual achievements, as

though Nature did not permit them to belong to both realms in equal degree. For every plus on one side must be paid for with a minus on the other.

Even within the limits of the natural individuation process, however, there are people who, entirely by themselves, without using special methods or needing any guidance, let alone the help of analysis, win to that wholeness and wisdom which are the fruit of a life consciously experienced and assimilated, all its battles fought. Or are there perhaps people who had a highly developed individuation granted them even in the cradle, as a gift of grace? Yet we know that among primitives no one can become a medicine-man or the wise man of the tribe without going through a hard lifelong discipline, that no saint is spared wrestling with his inner demons, and that no great artist ever accomplished his work without toil and sweat.

In view of these high demands it is not surprising that the majority of men follow the line of least resistance and confine themselves to the fulfilment of biological and material needs, and for the rest are intent on gaining the greatest possible number of pleasurable experiences. Most people look unremittingly for "happiness", and it never occurs to them that happiness is not the goal of life set them by the Creator. The true goal is a task that continues right up to life's evening, namely, the most complete and comprehensive development of the personality. It is this which gives life an incomparable value that can never be lost: inner peace, and therewith the highest form of "happiness".

But because man fears the mighty and continuous effort bound up with this task and if possible shuns every sacrifice, there are even in the "natural" individuation process all kinds of degeneracies and deformations. Precisely because it is naturebound, its manifestations may be "sick" and defective.[3] It may for instance be blocked (by psychosis), inhibited (by alcoholism or other cravings), it may be bogus, superficial, infantile, or prematurely interrupted (by death, accident, war), it may be hindered by degeneration, perversion, etc.

It is not the length of life and not its freedom from disturbances which are the decisive factors in the success of individuation but, as we have seen, the draining of life to the full, in the good and the difficult alike. Thus even a "short life", which compresses all the phases into a short time, can be brought to full maturity and rounded out, as we can see from numerous examples of outstanding personalities who were wise already in their youth. Among short lives, therefore, we have to distinguish between an individuation process that was broken off for some reason and remained incomplete, and one that is the result of a life lived to the full.[4]

The validity of man's psychic development considered as the "natural individuation process" in its manifold forms, and also as the subject of various psychological theories, is not called into question by Jung. His aim is rather to supplement and deepen the "way of nature", to ennoble it as it were, by demonstrating the possibility of an *opus contra naturam*. Or as Gerhard Adler has expressed it in a trenchant formula, "to resolve the thesis of pure nature and its antithesis of the opposing ego into the synthesis of *conscious* nature".[5]

What we are here concerned with is a deepening of the personality by a process adapted specifically to the nature of Western man, as is also attempted in other spheres of culture by corresponding rites and religious forms. Jung is not of the opinion, however, that alien cults and forms of religion should be taken over unheedingly by Western man. For example, he is against Europeans' practising yoga or indulging in other "mysteries" designed for totally alien psychic structures. They do not correspond to the European's state of consciousness and consequently lead him not to individuation but only into error.

The way of individuation, as understood by Jung, differs from the "natural" process, which simply "happens" to a man and of which he is the passive object, in that it is *followed and experienced consciously and is actively shaped by him*.[6] Between "I do" and "I am conscious of what I do" there is not only a vast difference but, at times, an outright opposition. As we know, the healthy man is healthy usually without being conscious of his healthiness. We see and hear a great variety of things all the time, we accept them without paying any particular attention to them, without performing the seeing and hearing as conscious acts. The senses perceive, and our consciousness takes cognizance of the perceived almost automatically, without knowingly integrating it. It is the same with our thinking, which often goes on spontaneously, without being consciously recognized as such and consciously elaborated. This is even truer of our actions. "Consequently there is a consciousness in which unconsciousness predominates, as well as a consciousness in which self-consciousness predominates." [7] Most people confuse self-reflection, the *sine qua non* of psychic development, with knowledge of their conscious ego-personality, although it is only by illuminating the unconscious psyche and relating to it that an apprehension of the complete personality becomes possible.

Jung lays great stress on the decisive role played by consciousness and its capacity for insight, though he rigorously rejects its dictatorship and constantly demands that attention be paid to the "messages" sent up from the unconscious depths. Work on the psyche in his view aims at giving these messages their due and, over and above that, at strengthening consciousness so that it shall be equal to the demands made upon it on the great journey of life, the "quest of the hero", through encounters with the contents of the unconscious.

It is therefore quite wrong to suppose that Jungian psychology recommends the exclusive observance of the voice that comes from the unconscious realms and announces itself, for example, in dreams. Statements like "I must get divorced" or "I must wind up this business" or "I must go to the United States because my dreams have told me to" are in complete opposition to Jung's view, unless the conscious standpoint coincides with what is suggested by the material coming from the unconscious. But when consciousness and the messages of the unconscious are in opposition, and no reconciliation is pos-

sible, the watchword is: Wait, persevere until a tolerable solution suddenly presents itself, as if it were a third possibility
that does justice to both sides. Whether it will be the "right"
one cannot of course be determined, but at least it will be in
harmony with the totality of the psyche, with the statements
made by both its realms, the conscious and the unconscious. At
bottom one never knows in advance whether one has done the
"right" thing. One must therefore be prepared to accept responsibility for everything one does, even if it should later
turn out that the "right" thing was the wrong one. But one
can only do that if one is always quite clear in advance about
the meaning and possible consequences of one's deeds. In this
sense it can be said that every conscious decision is at the same
time an ethical decision.

The peculiarity, then, of the second kind of individuation
process lies in the intervention of consciousness in the spontaneous, automatic flow of psychic life. An ethical decision is
sought, each time in the interests of developing what is singu-
lar or unique in the personality.

The Two Main Phases of the
Individuation Process

Both variants of the individuation process can be divided into two main phases containing numerous sub-divisions: that of the first and that of the second half of life. Each phase is the opposite of the other, but stands to it in a polar relationship. Their duration, the kind of task that has to be solved in them, and the depth and intensity of the experience vary with each individual. "At the stroke of noon the descent begins. And the descent means the reversal of all the ideals and values that were cherished in the morning,"[1] says Jung.

The transition from one phase to the other is of special importance. The "change of life" is a conflict between the onset of biological ageing, expressing itself in the psychic functions as well, and the urge and possibility for further spiritual and psychic development. It is a critical situation in which one has reached the zenith of life and, suddenly or gradually as the case may be, is then confronted with the reality of the end—death. Often a "balance account crisis" arises at this point.[2] The word "crisis" is very apt: it comes from the Greek, *krinein*, which means "to discriminate" and also "to decide". For here the great reversal takes place, which Charlotte Bühler has termed the "change of dominance", because it can give life an entirely new direction. Involuntarily one takes stock of one's assets in life, a sort of final reckoning is made regarding what

21

has been achieved and what has still to be achieved, and this results in an unmistakable credit and debit account. At the same time one sees equally clearly what was missed and should still be recovered, as well as all the things that can be recovered no longer. To look such truths in the eye is a test of courage. It demands insight into the necessity of growing old, and the courage to renounce what is no longer compatible with it. For only when one is able to discriminate between what must be discarded and what still remains as a valuable task for the future will one also be able to decide whether one is ready to strike out in the new direction consciously and positively. If the "change of dominance" fails to appear, the psyche knows no rest; it gets into a state of discontentment and uncertainty, finally ending in neurosis. Everything cries out for readjustment. That is why these years are rightly called the "change of life".

It is no longer disputed today that men as well can be subject to this change. Yet, though its effects in a man are often stronger than in a woman, they run their course as a rule only in the psychological realm. Although those affected may not care to admit it, they undergo during their "change of life" specific psychic—and often psychosomatic—disturbances characterized by increased lability, anxiety states of all kinds, depressions, crises of impotence, etc. Men find it even more difficult to accept growing old than women, for whom the menopause is something that can be neither kept secret nor got rid of nor reversed. Men fear the loss of virility, which they identify with vitality. This can drive them to the most astonishing antics and to all kinds of attempts to hang on to being young. They equate instinct, potency, and strength with their human value and their capacity to work, and their self-confidence becomes precarious even though this may not be immediately noticeable because of skilled disguises. There are, of course, exceptions, but they are fewer than one thinks. The picture of primitives who kill the leader of the tribe as soon as he is no longer capable of begetting progeny and has thus become totally useless still lives unconsciously in the soul of modern, civilized men and throws them into agitation.

Try as one may to turn a blind eye to growing old, sooner or later it can no longer be overlooked. Some sort of psychic readjustment becomes unavoidable if one does not wish to succumb to a neurosis. That is true of both forms of the individuation process, the "natural" and the "analytically assisted", and it is also true of both sexes. "To the psychotherapist an old man who cannot bid farewell to life appears as feeble and sickly as a young man who is unable to embrace it. And as a matter of fact, it is in many cases a question of the self-same infantile greediness, the same fear, the same defiance and wilfulness, in the one as in the other." [3]

Often the transition from the first to the second half of life is accompanied by other kinds of disturbances and serious upheavals. Divorce, change of profession, change of residence, financial losses, physical or psychic illnesses of all kinds characterize the readjustment or forcibly bring it about. Naturally a great deal depends on one's situation and on whether one is prepared in advance for the coming change. The less mature a person is when he reaches the change of life, the more powerfully the upheaval will affect him, provided of course that the change sets in at all and he does not remain stuck in an infantile or pubescent state; this can lead to a smouldering, chronic neurosis. There are indeed people—and perhaps they are in the majority—who slip into the second half of life slowly, almost unnoticeably. But they seldom attain the same broad maturity of personality as those who have to begin life's afternoon with much toil and suffering, and are thereby driven to an intensive reckoning between the ego and the unconscious components of the psyche. This also gives them a better chance to attain psychic wholeness. Hence difficulties in life, sudden entanglements, dangers and tests of courage, all of which have to be faced and conquered, form as it were an organic part of the analytical work.

These years of change should not be understood only as a

shifting of accent, but also, in the deepest sense of the word
"change", as a transformation. The extent, intensity, and duration of this transformation vary from individual to individual. Nevertheless, the discovery of a new life-form which goes
hand in hand with the successful conduct of life as a whole
depends on the degree to which a person is gripped by this
transformation, adopts a positive attitude towards it, and is
able to accomplish it. Very often the capacity for such a transformation does not depend on the objective bigness or small-
ness of the personality, but on the extension or "reconstruc-
tion" of its psychic "dimension". It is a question of moving
from an "ego-centred" [4] attitude to an "ego-transcending" [5]
one, in which the guiding principles of life are directed to
something objective, and this can be anything from one's children, one's house, one's work to the state, humanity, God.

The transformation can, according to Charlotte Bühler, be
either sudden or gradual. It can take place in a short time or
require several years. The greater the difference between the
initial and the end situation, that is, the greater the areas of
experience encompassed by the transformation, the more sudden it will be. On the other hand, the smaller this difference is,
the more gradually the transformation will take place. It then
has the character of a slow process of maturation and psychic
approfondissement.

The possibility of a maturation and rounding out of the
psyche is in principle inherent in every individual. Whether he
is able to accomplish it or not depends on the inhibiting factors which stud the path of man's outer and inner life. The
important thing is not the widened scope which consciousness
attains, but its "roundedness". In alchemy the "rotundum" is
a symbol of wholeness and completeness which expresses concretely what is meant in a metaphorical sense with reference to
the psyche. It is therefore a matter of indifference whether the
rotundum be a big or a little one; what alone matters is the
"roundedness", i.e., a state in which the greatest possible number of man's hidden qualities are made conscious, his psychic

capacities developed and condensed into a unity. This is a goal which generally can be reached—if at all—only in life's late evening.

Generally speaking one can say that whereas the first half of life is, in the nature of things, governed and determined by expansion and adaptation to outer reality, the second is governed by restriction or reduction to the essential, by adaptation to the inner reality. "Man has two aims," says Jung. "The first is the natural aim, the begetting of children and the business of protecting the brood; to this belongs the acquisition of money and social position. When this aim has been reached a new phase begins: the cultural aim." [6] "A young person has not yet acquired a past, therefore he has no present either. He does not create culture, he merely exists. It is the privilege and task of maturer people, who have passed the meridian of life, to create culture." [7] And one can add with Schopenhauer: "Life may be compared to a piece of embroidery, of which, during the first half of his time, a man gets a sight of the right side, and during the second half, of the wrong. The wrong side is not so pretty as the right, but it is more instructive; it shows the way in which the threads have been worked together." [8]

Once firmly anchored in one's profession, with the family founded and one's position in the outer world secured—a situation which applies primarily to the man and becomes acute for a woman only when house and home are in order and the children provided for—one is faced with the question: What now? What's all this leading to? For a moment, still veiled in the mists of the future, a premonition of the questionableness and transience of all existence rise up in one, something one had not thought of before. This question, growing ever louder, may present itself already at the end of the thirties. But once the forties are past, it becomes more and more urgent and is increasingly difficult to brush aside.[9] Naturally there are also people who even in their youth seek more for the meaning of life, for inner spiritual values, than for the external, the material, the earthly. They are the introverted, the seekers, the quiet and reflective ones, who nevertheless in the end feel they are the losers, because the promises of youth have flown away, because the first half of their life was actually lived under the sign of the second, a situation not lacking in tragedy. Many artists and scientists, however, have derived from such an unusual fate inspiration and strength for the creation of spiritually important work.

Much attention has been paid to the problems of the first half of life in scientific quarters, both theoretically and practically, during these last decades. Though they do not figure very prominently in Jung's work, the place they occupy in it is important. Frances Wickes[10] was the first of his pupils to venture into this territory, and since the Second World War she has been followed in England by Michael Fordham[11] and his pupil Eve Lewis,[12] in Israel by Erich Neumann,[13] and in Switzerland by the author,[14] who have all made independent contributions that explored new ground. Jung turned his researches principally to the psychological problems of the *second half of life,* which until recently had been unduly neglected by science. In the investigation of these phenomena as well as in the discovery of their meaning he acted as a pioneer.

When, therefore, he speaks of the individuation process as a gradual, conscious process of transformation, he has, though constantly bearing in mind the whole course of human life with its two great phases, in most cases tried to delineate it as a task for the years *following* the change of life.[15] This task should help people to give their lives a new meaning and should at the same time include a psychic preparation for death. "Seen in correct psychological perspective, death is not an end but a goal." [16] To confront this goal with the full force of the capacities for growth immanent in the psyche constitutes the real meaning of the second half of life and the highest dignity of man. Therefore Jung says: "In the secret hour of life's midday the parabola is reversed, death is born. The second half of life does not signify ascent, unfolding, increase, exuberance, but death, since the end is its goal. The negation of life's fulfilment is synonymous with the refusal to accept its ending. Both mean not wanting to live, and not wanting to live is identical with not wanting to die. Waxing and waning make one curve." [17]

Jung's psychology has repeatedly been attacked for having nothing to say to young people, and for being suited only for those who are already in the autumn of life. This seems unjustified when one considers his work as a whole. Besides the essays contained in his book *Psychologie und Erziehung*,[18] which are specifically devoted to the problems of the young, the valuable interpretations he has given of the symbols of the "divine child" [19] or of the *puer aeternus*,[20] the discovery of the archetypal background of the mother-child relationship, his observations on the development of the ego, on the role of introversion and extraversion[21] as well as of the functions of consciousness[22] in the development of young people, are all of fundamental importance for an understanding of, and therapeutic approach to, the conflicts of the first half of life. Jung constantly emphasizes that the overcoming of the tasks of youth is a prerequisite for psychic development during the second half. *Only then* is a person capable of submitting himself to the far-reaching process which the second half of life requires of him. The validity of this is apparent when a man who already stands on the threshold of the change of life has, with respect to his conscious personality, only reached the degree of development of an adolescent, a state of affairs that occurs more frequently than one thinks. In this case too the first requisite for maturation is the stability of the ego and the strengthening of consciousness, a typical task for the first half of life. *Only then* are the preconditions met for the venture which the second phase of the individuation process entails. This means that an eventual analysis must work with the viewpoints that apply to the first half of life even though the analysand is fifty years old but still possesses the psyche of a *puer aeternus*. In spite of his age he has no ego-stability and is miles away from the realities of life. So long as these defects are not removed it is better not to take too deep a plunge into the myth-haunted depths of the soul or to gallop away on a stout spiritual Pegasus—one could easily become the victim of inflation and lose the earth altogether from under one's feet.[23]

In our time this has become a particularly thorny problem. For the type of man who is intellectually developed but has remained affectively and emotionally a boy is a widespread phenomenon which is characteristic of our epoch, and which perhaps is connected with the emancipation of women in the twentieth century. The influence of the intellectually independent and mature woman, who in this way became a dominating force and often pushed the father's authority into the background, can have an exceedingly oppressive effect on her children, particularly on boys. One knows countless cases where this influence unconsciously and unwittingly prevented the development of the masculine ego to full responsibility. The man then remains fixated on the level of a pubescent, not infrequently has homosexual leanings, and remains a *puer aeternus*, an infantile adult, for the rest of his life. Alarming indeed, since often, if he is in an official position, he holds the fate of the world in his hands.

There are, of course, people who cannot be fitted into any category, exceptional people like artists, whose art often towers far above their personal development and who have something childish, youthful about them, or some physical weakness. These develop the individuation process in their work, instead of in the material of their own psyche. Maybe their constitution is inadequate, too sensitive to respond in the same way to both worlds, to their psyche and to their work. In many cases, therefore, it seems to make sense that some people should accomplish the individuation process on their own psyche, others in their artistic work, the work reflecting the process in its progressive unfolding and maturity. We can see this in the paintings of Rembrandt and Titian, in the writings of Goethe and Thomas Mann. The ego-personality of a great artist can, however, remain retarded; it is above all the medium through which inspiration is revealed and it is often formed under daemonic pressures. "Being essentially the instrument of his work, he is subordinate to it, and we have no right to expect him to interpret it for us. He has done his utmost by giving it form." [24] "How can we doubt that it is his art that explains the artist, and not the insufficiencies and conflicts of his personal life? These are nothing but the regrettable results of his being an artist, a man upon whom a heavier burden is laid than upon ordinary mortals. A special ability demands a greater expenditure of energy, which must necessarily leave a deficit on some other side of life." [25] "Great gifts are the fairest, and often the most dangerous, fruits on the tree of humanity. They hang on the weakest branches, which easily break." [26] "In most cases . . . the gift develops in inverse ratio to the maturation of the personality as a whole, and often one has the impression that a creative personality grows at the expense of the human being. Sometimes, indeed, there is such a discrepancy between the genius and his human qualities that one has to ask oneself whether a little less talent might not have been better." [27]

These quotations show what a ticklish thing it is we are dealing with. They shed light on the difficult problem of the unity or disunity of the artist's work and his personality, a problem that cannot be solved by any general rule. The longing to idealize the artist as an ordinary person too, to identify him with its "heroes", is deeply ingrained in the public. This idealized picture is passionately defended and the visible deviation from it, which so often occurs, is either sharply condemned or not taken notice of at all. Actually the real artist is outside all such categories. Geniuses are "monads", unique and unrepeatable phenomena, and every yardstick that is applied to them can easily become questionable.

For this reason the equally controversial question as to whether an artist should submit to being analyzed and whether analysis would conjure up a danger to his creativity can receive only an unsatisfactory answer and in no case an

exhaustive one. Presumably an artist will take refuge in analysis, if at all, only when the flow of his creative ideas dries up for
some reason, when he is cut off from the source of his images or
sounds and wants to get them moving again. But if his creative
powers are unbroken, a systematic realization of the unconscious contents of his psyche, such as occurs in an analytically
assisted individuation process, may not be indicated at all.

For unless the analysis is conducted very carefully with cat's-
paw sensitiveness, and if, for instance, the deeper-lying psychic
material is interpreted too rationalistically and too little room
is left for the symbol to live in, the conscious ego may then be
able to gain the ascendancy and enrich itself, thereby stopping
up the "porosity" of the psychic layers and inhibiting any
spontaneous productivity by too much criticism. In a properly
conducted analysis consciousness has to learn to tolerate contact with the contents rising up from below. In this matter
Freud and Jung were of the same opinion: if an artist cannot
stand analysis there is something wrong with his artistry. Jung
says: "True productivity is a spring that can never be stopped
up. Is there any trickery on earth which could have prevented
Mozart or Beethoven from creating? Creative power is might-
ier than its possessor. If it is not so, then it is a feeble thing,
and given favourable conditions will nourish an endearing talent, but no more . . . No breaking down of repressions can
ever destroy true creativeness." [28] Even when an artist had to go
through a severe psychic crisis—like Goya, Klee, or van Gogh
—the urge to create never let up. Would an analysis have been
any help? What a presumption that would be, to say the least!

The course of the first half of life has its own form and
follows its own laws, which one could describe as an "initiation
into adulthood" or an "initiation into outer reality". It forms
the first phase of the way of individuation. The operative factor behind both phases is the Self, that transconscious, central
authority of the psyche, which seems from the beginning to be
in *a priori* possession of the goal, and, with a kind of foreknowledge,[29] aims at the "entelechy, the unity and wholeness

of the human personality".[30] It is the organizing centre upon which all psychic phenomena depend, including the psychic course of life, the main features of which at this stage are the development of consciousness and the crystallization of the ego.

Emerging from the original psychic "unitary reality" [31] of inside and outside, from the identity of subject and object, the ego, in its encounter with the surrounding world, must grow together into a solid nucleus.[32] It must emancipate itself from the Self and from the absorptive powers of the collective psyche to the point where it becomes relatively self-contained. "For a moment I had the feeling that I carried a crystal in my heart, and I suddenly knew it was my ego." In this arresting image Hermann Hesse, in his novel *Demian*,[33] captures an experience which must be known to many young people.

The emancipation of the ego necessarily increases the distance and tension between the ego and the Self, so that often it comes to an actual "split". For when the ego, or conscious portion of the psyche, develops too one-sidedly and barricades itself against everything coming out of the unconscious, it may easily land itself in a kind of hypertrophy, in a rationalistic attitude cut off from the world of inner images and emotions. But for that very reason it calls them up and mobilizes them, because the self-regulating mechanism of the psyche immediately answers any one-sidedness with another one-sidedness. If this attitude continues or gets stronger, it involves considerable psychic dangers. A feeling of emptiness, isolation, insecurity is the result, with corresponding neuroses. But it is no less menacing if, by contrast, the ego remains weak and fragmentary and does not achieve independence, for it may then fall a defenceless victim to uncontrollable impulses and ideas and be inundated and extinguished by a flood of unconscious contents. When that happens, one is well on the way to a psychosis.

These dangers may be guarded against by a circumspect endeavour to consolidate the ego and broaden the field of con-

sciousness. Careful work on his dreams and a systematic enlargement of his knowledge can help the analysand to gain a
greater capacity and readiness for experience. At any rate, once
he has set foot on the path of an analytically assisted individuation process he must summon up a positive attitude and spare
himself no effort. Unfortunately it frequently happens that,
with the best will in the world, no co-operation follows from
the unconscious, and that an insurmountable resistance pre-
vents any progress. This is found chiefly with pathological
cases, with people whose psychic balance is constantly about to
tip over. Nevertheless, in Jung's view, even in such cases patient work on the psyche is indicated, for it can be extremely
helpful.

Even schizophrenia can be viewed in the context of the individuation process. Jung sees it as an attempt at individuation
going on in itself, without the participation of consciousness;
as an ever-repeated, fruitless attempt of the unconscious to
force the conscious mind, by the very intensity of the archetypal images and motifs, to understand and assimilate them,
and thus to free the individual from the pressure of menacing
unconscious contents. Those who become schizophrenics, one
might say, are people whose ego is too weak and whose psychic
background is too explosive, so that its contents cannot be
worked through by the ego. Jung says: "At bottom we discover
nothing new and unknown in the mentally ill; rather, we encounter the substratum of our own natures." [34] Further:
". . . psychiatry, in the broadest sense, is a dialogue between
the sick psyche and the psyche of the doctor, which is presumed
to be 'normal' ".[35] And elsewhere: "It is a fact that psychological preparation in schizophrenia results in a better prognosis. I
therefore make it a rule to let those threatened with schizophrenia, or mild schizophrenics or latent schizophrenics, have
as much psychological knowledge as possible, because I know
from experience that there is then a greater chance of their
getting out of the psychotic interval again. Equally, psychological enlightenment after a psychotic attack is in certain condi-

tions extraordinarily helpful . . . I would always recommend psychological education as a prophylactic measure with schizoids. Like neurosis, psychosis too in its inner course is a process of individuation, but one that is not associated with consciousness and runs on like an *ouroboros*[36] in the unconscious. Psychological preparation links the process with consciousness, or rather, there is the possibility of such a connection and hence of a curative effect." [37]

The Stages

THE individuation process, as the way of development and maturation of the psyche, does not follow a straight line, nor does it always lead onwards and upwards. The course it follows is rather "stadial", consisting of progress and regress, flux and stagnation in alternating sequence. Only when we glance back over a long stretch of the way can we notice the development. If we wish to mark out the way somehow or other, it can equally well be considered a "spiral", the same problems and motifs occurring again and again on different levels. Erich Neumann described the individuation process as an interior Odyssey which he called "centroversion". Jung spoke of it as a "labyrinthine" path, and said of it that the longest way is at the same time the shortest.

If we now set out to observe and describe this way in its various stages, we can on the one hand do so with reference to the development of the basic typological characteristics of the individual as established by Jung; in other words, we can describe it as the progressive differentiation of his attitudinal and functional modes of being. We can, on the other hand, consider it in terms of the symbolism of the most important figures that manifest themselves along this way, and describe it as the systematic confrontation, step by step, between the ego and the contents of the unconscious.

The development of the ego demanded during the first half of life, stage by stage, must run parallel with the differentiation of the individual's attitude and of the constitutionally predominant function of consciousness, as well as with a corresponding expansion of the field of consciousness and the formation of a suitable "persona",[1] if the ego is to achieve a stability that is at once elastic and capable of resistance.

Jung distinguishes two types of attitude in relation to the object: extraversion and introversion. The first is oriented by the object, the second by the subjective impression which the object releases. Both types are inherent in the psychic structure of the individual, but one of them is congenitally predominant and, by its preferential use, marks the type of character. The other, unused or used only rarely, remains more or less undeveloped and unconscious, but comes to the surface in a more or less inferior form as soon as the threshold of consciousness sinks. Whenever this sinking occurs, whenever our attention slackens and consciousness is no longer concentrated, i.e., when we become distracted, we notice that all sorts of ways of behaving, associations or ideas which are normally suppressed rise up and forcibly obtrude themselves on us. We may, for instance, be reading a book word for word and suddenly notice that we are occupied with quite irrelevant thoughts and no longer remember what we have read. The stronger and solider the ego is, therefore, the better it will be able to withstand or resist these intruders.

The same is true of the functions of consciousness: thinking, feeling, sensation, intuition. Jung has described them as the four "modes of apprehension" by which the ego takes in and assimilates the material coming from without and within. Here again there is one main function which is as a rule congenital and is the most clearly differentiated. Of the other three, two are less conscious, the so-called "auxiliary functions", and one is the "inferior function", which is the most closely associated with the unconscious. They too take part in the assimilation of material from outside and inside. But as consciousness and unconsciousness are not constants but are in continual interplay—one may even speak of a "sliding scale" [2] between the full luminosity and complete obfuscation of consciousness—the main attitude and the main function have only "predominantly" the leading role. Again and again the other, less developed modes of behaviour can come into play. This shows itself in the sometimes kaleidoscopic change of our moods, in the fluctuation of attention, and in the lability of our psychic manifestations, when, under the pressure of circumstances, the other components of the psyche appear alongside the ruling and differentiated ones. That is why Jung's typology gives admirable expression to the ceaseless, dynamic mobility of the psyche; it is fundamentally different from all other type theories, which are related only to consciousness.

As the four functions of consciousness can, depending on the "attitude-type", be either introverted or extraverted, we have eight basic types, which seldom appear in pure form. Usually one meets them in any number of transitional and mixed forms. The development of the individual type to relative strength and stability takes place also in the course of the natural individuation process, but can be accelerated and intensified in the analytically assisted process, side by side with the expansion of the field of consciousness.

If a person avails himself all his life only of a single—the main—function, there is a danger of neurotic disturbances arising from the partial or complete repression of the other functions, and the same is true of the "attitude-type". It is no less a matter for misgiving when none of the functions is properly differentiated, that is, when they all remain at the adolescent level. This may be taken as a symptom of retarded ego-development. If it continues, it leads as much as the other to serious psychic complications. In such cases, the person concerned remains without a standpoint, torn between extremes like so many adolescents. The differentiation of "attitude" and "function", according to the person's age—first the dominant ones, and then in later years the others that have been too little used—is therefore a criterion for the successful course of the individuation process. From this it can be seen what station of the way he has reached.

By the "persona" Jung means that segment of the ego which is concerned with relations to the surrounding world. Its task is to build up a relatively stable façade adapted to the demands of present-day civilization. An elastic persona that "fits well" belongs to the psychic wardrobe of the adult man, and its lack or its rigidity is an indication of psychic maldevelopment. Contrariwise, there is always some danger of identifying with the persona, e.g., the professor with his textbooks, the tenor with his voice, the general with his rank. Then one can no longer do anything in a human way, one is glued to one's mask. But if one has no proper persona, one strikes other people as vague and vacillating, and no one knows what to make of such an individual. Jung writes: "One could say, with a little exaggeration, that the persona is that which in reality one is not, but which oneself as well as others think one is." [3] If the persona is lacking, one has no protecting "face", and is exposed to the world with all one's moods like a child.

As the persona, if it is one that "fits well", makes use of the predominant attitude and function, it grows and consolidates itself at the same rate as they do. This gives it the suppleness it needs if it is to maintain itself without robbing the psychic qualities that lie "behind" it of their vitality. The persona can be chosen only up to a certain point. It is formed by a successful union of the ego-ideal, i.e., what one imagines one ideally is, with the ideal of the surrounding world and what it expects of one. If the persona is unable to do justice to one of these factors, it will not function properly and often acquires an unnatural, neurotic aspect.

The development and differentiation of the predominant "attitude" and main "function" as well as of the persona generally go hand in hand with experiences and conflicts which are indispensable for the maturation of the psyche. They broaden a man's knowledge of himself and of life and in that way extend the scope of his consciousness.

A "rounding out" of the psyche is not yet called for at this stage of development; indeed, a certain degree of one-sidedness is still necessary and valuable. It gives a young person the verve and initiative he needs in order to attain independence and weather the inner and outer storms which accompany his psychic growth. The unreflecting activity and spontaneity that carry him along help him to win his position in the world; though they entail the drawback of unconsciousness, they supply the drive and push needed in the struggle for existence.

During the first half of life there is also formed, as a result of the necessarily one-sided development of consciousness, the *shadow*, which is the sum of all the qualities conforming to our sex that were neglected or rejected while the ego was being built up. The growth of the shadow, like that of the persona, keeps pace with that of the ego; it is, as it were, the ego's mirror-image, and is compounded partly of repressed, partly of unlived psychic features which, for moral, social, educational, or other reasons, were from the outset excluded from consciousness and from active participation in life and were therefore repressed or split off. Accordingly the shadow can be marked by both positive and negative qualities.

Besides the "personal shadow" there is in Jung's view also a "collective shadow" in which the general evil is contained (as in the figure of Mephistopheles, for instance). It gives expression not to the contents belonging to the personal life-history of the individual but to everything negative, everything that opposes the spirit of the time, and represented in the Christian Middle Ages, for instance, by witches and sorcerers. Even today, the qualities of the collective shadow are imputed either to capitalism or to communism, according to one's political beliefs.

The shadow qualities may appear personified in dreams. They often appear in projection, as the qualities of some object or person with whom there is a correspondingly strong positive or negative tie. Mostly they are projected on persons of the same sex as the projicient, as can be observed among brothers and sisters or pairs of friends (this is particularly striking in homosexual relationships). When we lose conscious control of ourselves for one reason or another, the qualities of the shadow appear on our own persons, in the form of blunders, asocial behaviour, egoisms, rudeness, etc., which can no longer be projected and show that there are other powers in us besides the ego.

People who believe their ego represents the whole of their psyche, and who neither know nor want to know all the other qualities that belong to it, are wont to project their unknown "soul parts" into the surrounding world—for everything unconscious is first experienced in projection, as qualities of objects. These are those well-known people who always think they are in the right, who in their own eyes are quite blameless and wonderful, but always find everybody else difficult, malicious, hateful, and the source of all their troubles. Nobody likes to admit his own darkness, for which reason most people put up—even in analytical work—the greatest resistance to the realization of their shadow. As Ulrich Zwingli long ago remarked very aptly: "Like an octopus hiding behind its black juice to avoid seizure, a man, so soon as he observes we will be at him, suddenly envelops himself in such a dense hypocritical fog that the sharpest eye cannot perceive him . . . His impudence in lying, his readiness to deny and disown, is so great that, when you think you have laid hold of him, he has already slipped out by the back door." 4

We learn by experience, mostly unpleasant, through collisions of all kinds, through disappointments and illnesses, that we as much as other people have shadow qualities. This insight leads to self-knowledge, which has always been considered the supreme spiritual goal, as witnessed by tradition. Schiller, too, describes in his poem, "The Veiled Image at Sais",5 how the great secret, hidden from him all his life, was himself, his own "truth", which he suddenly recognized in this image; from that moment:

> . . . gone
> Was all the former gladness of his life,
> And sorrow bore him to an early grave.

The ego and its antagonist, the shadow, represent an archetypal motif that plays a role not only in our daily life, but also for instance in mythology. The "twins" or "unlike brothers", such as Castor and Pollux (the Dioscuri), the Mithraic Cautes and Cautopates, Gilgamesh and his friend Enkidu, Apollo and his brother Dionysus, illustrate this bi-polar relationship as also do Cain and Abel, Jacob and Esau, etc. We meet them again in literature as Don Quixote and Sancho Panza, Dante and Virgil, Faust and Wagner, etc. The sacred physicians Cosmas and Damian exemplify the same motif. As they form a pair of opposites which taken together constitute a "whole", healing power is attributed to them. And indeed experience confirms that the conscious realization of the shadow, the disclosure of its qualities, and the integration of its contents always have a therapeutic effect because this is a step on the way towards man's wholeness.

The concept of integration involves more than a mere knowledge of the shadow's qualities. For example an alcoholic, in order to be cured, must not only be conscious of his tendency or compulsion to drink—which many of them deny—but must also discover the deeper reasons that have induced his craving. These reasons are always shadow qualities which he cannot accept, which he flees from in order to rid himself of the pangs of conscience their recognition would entail. The precondition for a cure, therefore, is that the alcoholic should keep these shadow qualities constantly before him, seeing in his mind's eye this drinker in himself as his unswerving companion, until he can no longer forget his presence. For "a content can be integrated only when its double aspect has become conscious and when it is grasped not merely intellectually but understood according to its feeling value".[6] Only then has he accepted it completely and integrated it as his own possession and so gained power over it. Truly a task which one fears, understandably enough; for fulfilling it means nothing less than sharing the life of one's antagonist, who may be dark or light, evil or good, but will always be undifferentiated, undeveloped, and unadapted. This is not surprising as he spends his whole life, so to speak, "in Coventry".

During the first phase of the individuation process, which properly comes to an end with the crystallization of the ego, one should, according to Jung, have recourse to analytical assistance only if there are special therapeutic or "fateful" reasons for it. Such is the case, for instance, when there is a psychic complication, a special fear of life, a neurosis, or a difficult situation which cuts the individual off from the natural and necessary experiences and trials of life or imposes on him a burden he is unable to carry alone.

In general, if there are difficulties in the first half of life an analysis of the repressed "ontogenetic" contents (i.e., those pertaining to the life-history of the individual) is sufficient. They correspond roughly to the problems of childhood and youth considered by Freud, and for this reason Jung too, in such cases, would take account of the Freudian viewpoints, though giving them rather a different accent. Hard-and-fast rules cannot, of course, be made. With younger people one can usually manage with Freudian and Adlerian aims and help them to adapt to the circumstances of their lives. But with people over forty this is no longer true in the majority of cases. "The basic facts of the psyche undergo a very marked alteration in the course of life, so much so that we could almost speak of a psychology of life's morning and a psychology of its afternoon." [7] Hence in analytical work very much depends on the age of the patient and naturally also on the kind of material his associations and dreams present.

Usually it is easier for an extravert to adapt to the demands of outer reality—the specific task of the first half of life—than it is for an introvert, whose nature is moulded rather by his inner experiences. This frequently leads to difficulties with adaptation and even to neurotic disturbances. In the nature of things the introvert will feel drawn to the "inward way". But as this way presupposes a stable ego, the acquisition of which is particularly difficult for the introvert because of his fear of concrete reality, it is chiefly introverts who resort to psychotherapeutic help in the first half of life.

Just as the tasks of the first half of life present difficulties to the introvert, those of the second are a particularly thorny problem for the extravert. The successful extravert who has remained one-sided will frequently notice, when he approaches the afternoon of life, that he is dried up inside, just as the inveterate introvert, when he is getting on in years, cannot fail to recognize that he has really missed half his life in the outer world. Both then realize that the inner anchor is lacking which would hold them steady in face of the ever-nearing reality of their life's end.

At this point the second phase of the individuation process begins, when the ego, having become consolidated during the first phase, turns back in order to gather new vitality from contact with its origin, the creative background of the psyche, and to cast anchor in it this time for sure. After having broken away from the domain of the Self, the ego must re-establish a connection with it so as not to remain rootless and lifeless. "The goal of psychic development is the self. There is no linear evolution; there is only a circumambulation of the self. Uniform development exists, at most, only at the beginning; later, everything points towards the centre." [8] In this sense one can regard the individuation process as a growing of the ego out of the Self and as a re-rooting in it.

This turning-point, which normally begins with the transition from the first to the second half of life, cannot be pinned down to a definite year or to a definite period, but varies from individual to individual. It summons up the more or less unconscious, hitherto neglected sides of the psyche. Unless they participate in life and become relatively differentiated, the wholeness the individuation process is striving for cannot be reached, although it is, of course, quite impossible to bring all the repressed and unlived material to light, as well as all four "functions" in equal degree, and make it accessible to consciousness. The neurotic and psychotic breakdowns of this period are often due, according to Jung, to the inability to follow up the demand for conscious realization; they are crises pertaining to the change of life and are *not* the result of problems in childhood. In most of the cases the lack of a tenable philosophy of life or of a religious foundation is also apparent— which, in this critical phase, when everything gets unsettled and needs to be built up again, would provide a secure foothold. As a rule there is no proper relationship to the suprapersonal as a support, so that the crises are due to actual conflicts in the present and not to those rooted in the past.

Practical work in the individuation process centres on the observation of dreams and fantasies, the interpretation of their imagery with the help of the method of amplification,[9] and the distinction between their personal and their archetypal aspects. This work can result not only in the removal of the crisis but also in an activation of the creative powers of the unconscious psyche. By confronting the long repressed contents of the unconscious the ego is able to objectify them so that they can now be recognized and understood. There is no conscious realization without discrimination of the intrapsychic opposites. "The essential thing is to differentiate oneself from these unconscious contents by personifying them, and at the same time to bring them into relationship with consciousness. That is the technique for stripping them of their power. It is not too difficult to personify them, as they always possess a certain degree of autonomy, a separate identity of their own. Their autonomy is a most uncomfortable thing to reconcile oneself to, and yet the very fact that the unconscious presents itself in that way gives us the best means of handling it." [10] "Conscious and unconscious stand in a reciprocal, dynamic relationship; out of the unconscious rise contents and images, and they show themselves to the conscious mind as though secretly asking to be grasped and understood, so that 'birth' may be accomplished and 'being' created," says Aniela Jaffé. "If consciousness fails, the images sink back again into the dark, into nothingness, and everything remains as if unhappened. But if it succeeds in grasping the meaning of the images, a transformation takes place, and not merely of consciousness in the sense of an expansion or an illumination, but, strangely enough, of the unconscious as well; there is an activation of the 'nothingness'." [11]

Whereas the psychic features pertaining to the shadow derive from the personal life-history of the individual, and their conscious realization is the task of an analysis in the first half of life, one of the main tasks of the second phase of the individuation process—unless there are exceptional reasons against having to penetrate into the deeper transpersonal layers of the psyche—is a confrontation with the unconscious feminine features of the man, which Jung calls the *anima,* or with the unconscious masculine features of the woman, the *animus.*[12] Both are archetypal powers and besides personal elements also contain collective ones. Being so constituted, they form the natural bridge to the deepest layers of the psyche.

We find ourselves confronted with the figures of anima and animus either in the outer world (when they are projected on persons) or in dreams and fantasies. In this respect they behave just like the shadow. In addition, they are embodied in mythology and art, in legend and fairytale, by figures known to everyone, and their manifestations include every conceivable quality of man and woman, from the lowest to the highest. Their first representatives, for the child, are father and mother in their everyday reality. Yet, as Jung has shown from the dreams of earliest childhood, the child brings into the world with him an *a priori* knowledge, unconscious at first, of the paternal and maternal as perpetually repeated, archetypal forms of being. The individual component and the collective ground-plan immanent as a structural element of the psyche together constitute that psychic image which we call "mother" or "father" and which, as we have said, represents the earliest form of anima or animus.

In the first half of life it is natural and logical that these intrapsychic figures should appear in projection, and that we are thus attracted to the men and women who are their carriers, and fall in love with them. The projection produces a mutual attraction, it is the "trap" that embroils us with the other sex and so ensures the continuation of the species. Conversely, it is the task of the second half of life to withdraw the projections. It belongs to the second phase of the individuation process, when a man must learn to stand by himself, to discover the contrasexual element in himself and to fecundate it, thus rounding out his personality without impairing his faculty for relationship as such. If the "bodily child" is born of the first form of relationship, the fruit of the second is the "spiritual child". That is why we can observe that creative, spiritually productive people are often congenitally endowed with a relatively large share of contrasexual features, that they are "hermaphroditic" by psychic constitution, so to speak, and, as a result, not infrequently exhibit "narcissistic" tendencies.

The encounter with anima and animus makes it possible for us to apprise ourselves of our contrasexual traits in all their manifestations and to accept at least a part of the qualities projected on the male or female partner as belonging to our own selves, though as a rule this is not accomplished without violent resistances. What man will recognize or accept his moodiness, his unreliability, his sentimentality, and all the other allegedly "feminine" vices, as his own characteristics instead of chalking them up to the nearest female in his vicinity? And what woman will be persuaded to admit that her immovable opinions and arguments are begotten by a bogus logic which stems from her own unconscious masculinity? Once they are made conscious and are no longer projected, but are experienced as belonging to oneself, as realities and agencies within the psyche, anima and animus become symbols of its power to procreate and to give birth: everything new and creative owes its existence to them. They are the fount from which all artistic productivity flows.

In the course of further development, it is necessary to delineate the experience of these masculine or feminine traits more sharply, to separate what is individual and unique in the man or woman from the collective foundation of the psyche as well as from the external collective situation. Expressed in the language of symbols, this means adding a depth-dimension to the archetypal figures of the "Fatherly" and "Motherly" that appear at the beginning of life. Jung speaks of them, in this later, differentiated phase of the individuation process, as the "Wise Old Man" and the "Great Mother", principles of the primordial, masculine, spiritual Logos and of the primordial, feminine, earthly Eros. Their realization brings final detachment from the concrete parents. The conflicts with father and mother, the relations with them, which occupy a central place in Freudian theory, play—in Jung's psychology—a decisive role only in an analysis during the first half of life; in the second, once they are worked through, they become the gateway into the "realm of the Mothers", the collective unconscious.[13]

For once a man has reached a certain state of maturity through the individuation process it becomes possible for him to see his apparently insurmountable personal problems in the light of objective problems common to all humanity, and this not infrequently robs them of their urgency and their sting. "What, on a lower level, had led to the wildest conflicts and to panicky outbursts of emotion, now looks like a storm in the valley seen from the mountain top. This does not mean that the storm is robbed of its reality, but instead of being in it one is above it." [14] One is no longer directly affected by it, having gained the necessary detachment.

The meeting with the "primordial images" is not without its dangers, because the archetypal motifs which are constellated by the analytical work, if it goes deep enough, prove to be charged with a powerful numinosity.[15] Not for nothing is the individuation process said to be an analogy of the "quest of the hero", or of the dangers which he must overcome before he can gain the king's throne. In this phase of the work it is no exaggeration to say that the ego enters the realm of those figures which, in Jung's commentary on the *Tibetan Book of the Dead,* are called the "devouring, blood-drinking gods" who conjure up the danger of psychosis.[16] The archetypal material that comes up is the same as that of which the delusions of the insane are composed.[17] The shattering effect of these borderline phenomena, of these inner experiences and confrontations, brings about a transformation which enables the matured personality to take the "middle way" and finally win to psychic peace. That such an undertaking requires a strong and resilient ego, and also, if all the dangers are to be overcome, the constant surveillance of a skilled and perceptive therapist with a stable personality, should need no further stressing.

The confrontation with the shadow and its integration must always be achieved first in the individuation process in order to strengthen the ego for further laps in the journey and for the crucial encounter with the Self. That is why the shadow qualities must first be made conscious, even at the risk of neglecting other aspects and other figures presented by the psychic material. We find the same thing in myths and fairytales, where the hero always needs a friend, his own shadow side, as a companion in order to overcome the dangers of his quest. Ego and shadow together form that comprehensive consciousness which alone is able to meet and come to terms with the archetypal powers, and the contrasexual figures in particular.

The sequence of archetypal symbols that are constellated in the course of the analytical work, and the conscious confrontation with them, should not be imagined as a normative process which remains constantly the same. The principle is unchanging—namely, to pay attention to whatever the depths may present; only the accent, the interpretation one gives the material, changes according to situation and age. In the first half of life the material of the collective unconscious is neglected in favour of that from the personal unconscious; in the second it is the other way round. Generally speaking, the shadow blocks the view of the other figures in the psyche so long as it is not differentiated from the ego, and the same is true of anima and animus. So long as they remain undifferentiated, the field of consciousness is not broad enough to accommodate the other archetypal images and figures with their particular dynamism.

Ego and Self

THE aim of the individuation process is a synthesis of all partial aspects of the conscious and unconscious psyche. It seems to point to an ultimately unknowable, transcendent "centre" of the personality, which—paradoxically—is at the same time its periphery—and is of the "highest intensity", possessing an extraordinary power of irradiation. This centre and periphery Jung calls the *Self*, and he terms it the origin and fulfilment of the ego.

It appears to be the origin of the ego because the ego, as a "part" of the Self, is the centre of the field of consciousness through which alone we experience and perceive. Everything that does not pass through the ego is "unconscious", not known to us. The degree to which the ego is affected by its perceptions varies, and the luminosity of consciousness, i.e., the sharpness of its focus and its powers of assimilation, will vary accordingly. The ego is, however, also the "fulfilment" of the Self, since it is the only authority in the psyche which can know of the Self, relate to it, and remain in constant, living connection with it. A strong, consolidated ego is fed not only by the material of consciousness but also from the source of the Self, having a share in both realms.

Jung explains the relation of ego to Self as follows: "The term 'self' seemed to me a suitable one for this unconscious substrate, whose actual exponent in consciousness is the ego. The ego stands to the self as the moved to the mover, or as object to subject, because the determining factors which radiate out from the self surround the ego on all sides and are therefore supraordinate to it. The self, like the unconscious, is an *a priori* existent out of which the ego evolves. It is, so to speak, an unconscious prefiguration of the ego." [1] It is more encompassing than the ego, which is as it were the executive organ within the great sphere of the self. "When I call this unknowable thing the self," Jung says elsewhere,[2] "nothing has happened except that the operations of the unknowable have received a comprehensive name. But this is not to prejudge its content. A large unknown portion of my own being is included in it, but, because this portion is unconscious, I cannot indicate its extent and its boundaries. The self is therefore a *borderline concept,* which is far from being covered by the known psychic processes."

The Self is always there, it is the central, archetypal, structural element of the psyche, operating in us from the beginning as the organizer and director of the psychic processes. Its *a priori* teleological character, its striving to realize an aim, exist even without the participation of consciousness. Although the infantile ego grows out of the Self, it is at first unconscious of this fact; many people remain unconscious of it all their lives, and this harbours considerable dangers. Either the Self then appears in projection and meets us as an alien thing attached to some external object, or else it produces an inflation of the ego, because the ego is then not separated from the figures in the unconscious and is still wholly contained in the Self, identical with it, which amounts to megalomania. But if the Self is withdrawn from projection and recognized as something operative in ourselves, if it is understood as an autonomous reality and is differentiated from the other psychic elements, "then one is truly one's own yea and nay. The self then functions as a union of opposites and thus constitutes the most immediate experience of the Divine which it is psychologically possible to imagine." [3] It then represents the unity in which all psychic opposites cancel out.

Its inherent metaphysical aspect, its fateful character, give the Self a godlike power in the psyche. It is only natural, therefore, that Jung should draw parallels between the images in which the Self becomes visible and can be perceived by us and those in which God appears. This had led many people, above all theologians, to the mistake of thinking that with his concept of the Self Jung wanted to give God himself a name, although time and again in his writings he has emphasized that his statements about the Self refer only to the manifestation of the God-image and of the God-concept in the human psyche. "At all events," Jung says, "the soul must contain in itself the faculty of relationship to God, i.e., a correspondence, otherwise a connection could never come about. *This correspondence is, in psychological terms, the archetype of the God-image.*" [4] Since God-images are the products of religious fantasy they are unavoidably anthropomorphic and therefore, like every symbol, capable of psychological elucidation. But psychology can make no statements about the nature of God. On the other hand, it can very well observe and describe the phenomenology of his "reflection" in the human psyche, and explore it scientifically.

Jung has repeatedly explained that psychology, as an empirical science, is not competent to do more than establish whether the factor found in the psyche may, on the basis of comparative research, legitimately be termed a "God-image". "Nothing positive or negative has thereby been asserted about the possible existence of God, any more than the archetype of the 'hero' posits the actual existence of a hero." [5] "In physics we can do without a God-image, but in psychology it is a definite fact that has got to be reckoned with, just as we have to reckon with 'affect', 'instinct', 'mother', etc. It is the fault of the everlasting contamination of object and image that people can make no conceptual distinction between 'God' and 'God-image', and therefore think that when one speaks of the 'God-

image' one is speaking of God and offering 'theological' explanations. It is not for psychology, as a science, to demand an
hypostatization of the God-image. But, the facts being what
they are, it does have to reckon with the existence of a God-
image." [6] "The idea of God is an absolutely necessary psychological function of an irrational nature, which has nothing
whatever to do with the question of God's existence. The human intellect can never answer this question, still less give any
proof of God. Moreover such proof is superfluous, for the idea
of an all-powerful divine Being is present everywhere, unconsciously if not consciously, because it is an archetype." [7]
" 'God' is a primordial experience of man, and from the remotest times humanity has taken inconceivable pains either to
portray this baffling experience, to assimilate it by means of interpretation, speculation, and dogma, or else to deny it. And
again and again it has happened, and still happens, that one
hears too much about the 'good' God and knows him too well,
so that one confuses him with one's own ideas and regards
them as sacred because they can be traced back a couple of
thousand years. This is a superstition and an idolatry every bit
as bad as the Bolshevist delusion that 'God' can be educated
out of existence." [8]

The transcendent God will remain the object primarily of
theology and faith, but his operation in the depths of the
psyche, as the "immanent God", is also the concern of scientific
psychology, since he can make himself known directly through
the symbols of the Self. People do not listen to their inner
voice, however; only a few are able to believe that something
divine is contained in their soul. "Christian education has
done all that is humanly possible, but it has not been enough.
Too few have experienced the divine image as the innermost
possession of their own souls." [9] "If the theologian really be-
lieves in the almighty power of God on the one hand and in the
validity of dogma on the other, why then does he not trust God
to speak in the soul? Why this fear of psychology? Or is, in
complete contradiction to dogma, the soul itself a hell from

which only demons gibber?" [10] Although the Bible says "The kingdom of God is within you," [11] most people seek it only outside. Nevertheless, from the encounter with the "immanent God" the "transcendent God" can be spontaneously inferred, for the God-images "imprinted" in the psyche, the symbols of the Self, logically presuppose an "imprinter". God can naturally be outside as well as inside. He is everywhere, but it is only in the psyche that his workings can be perceived through the symbols of the Self.

If the ego ceases to be at death, then it ceases to be aware of the existence of the Self and can no longer establish a relationship with it. The God-images are then extinguished; the manifestations of the Self perish with the ego. Whether the divine essence, reflected and manifested in the living soul, continues to exist independently of the individual, timelessly and nonspatially, is again a question of belief and not a matter for scientific investigation.

It is one of the foremost tasks of the individuation process to raise the God-images, that is their radiations and effects, to consciousness and thus establish a constant dynamic contact between the ego and the Self. This alliance bridges over the tendencies to personality dissociation which arise from the instincts pulling in opposite directions.

Erich Neumann has called the relation between ego and Self an "axis", because the whole development of the personality revolves round it and is inherent in the psyche from the very beginning. Not only the development of the ego and of consciousness, but every change or transformation of the individual is, according to him, accomplished with the help of this ego-Self axis.[12] At first, in childhood, and often long afterwards, sometimes even till death, the ego is unconscious of its relation to the Self. Only when it has become conscious of it as a living thing is the reciprocal action between ego and Self established, only then does the axis function in a dynamic way and give the individual an inner certainty and feeling of security, as though he were contained in an all-embracing whole. It amounts to "a quasi-conscious or supra-conscious, at any rate no longer un-conscious, experience that world and psyche, outside and in-side, above and below are only two aspects of a unity sundered by consciousness", says Neumann.[13]

This axis is the vehicle also for the formation and develop-ment of consciousness, without which God may perhaps be "felt" but cannot be perceived in his manifestations. Wherever we may encounter God, we shall be able to apprehend him only with the help of our human, limited psychic structure, which is our "receiving apparatus". His real essence can, of course, never be grasped within the confines of the psyche, since it transcends them; at most it can be divined when we meet it in the images and symbols of the Self, or when it re-veals itself to faith. Always the plenitude of the divine radi-ance has to pass through the filter of our human nature and reaches us obscured and refracted.

What Jung speaks about, therefore, is always only the "re-flection"—the imagery in which God, the inapprehensible, portrays and communicates himself to us. Truth and life can be grasped only in similitudes, and the twofold task of man is to "perceive the unearthly in the earthly, to give it earthly form in work, word . . . and deed; this is the essence of the true symbol",[14] and hence also of the Self as the reflection of the unearthly, the ineffable.

This reflection, this image indwelling in the human heart from time immemorial, expresses that virtual centre in the psyche which possesses the greatest charge of energy. Every con-tent that is anywhere near this supercharged centre receives from it a numinous power, as though "possessed" by it. Again and again man has experienced that from this centre he could sense God's workings in his psyche at their most overwhelming, that "the voice of transcendence resounds through it".[15] And as often as he put another content in his centre in place of God—whether it were a beloved partner, money, nation, party, or any other "ism"—and made it a surrogate for God, he became its victim to his own destruction.

In a psyche that is "in order" the various psychic components balance one another and are grouped round the centre. If it is not the God-image but another content that occupies this centre, the content gets blown up with the accumulation of energy, often to bursting point. The God-image is then thrust aside from its rightful place, loses its efficacy, and can become so etiolated that it vanishes from consciousness altogether. The result is loss of psychic balance, leading to neurosis or psychosis. For it is then no longer a knowledge of God, his influence, that possess the individual, but the content he has put in the psychic centre instead of the God-image.

A man "possessed" is always a religious person in the negative sense, so to speak. He does not notice that, for sheer terror of "falling into the hands of the living God", he has sold himself body and soul to God's devilish counterpart. For the Self, too, has a shadow, a dark half, like everything human. "In the empirical self, light and shadow form a paradoxical unity," says Jung.[16] When the occupant of the psychic centre is smaller than the God-image, or when this centre is still walled in by convention or petrified beliefs, void within and ruled by fear, the relationship to the God-image is at an end, the ego-Self axis broken. Either the ordering consciousness is then separated by a deep rift from the dark powers of the unconscious psyche, now become autonomous, each of them going its own way and involving the individual in a labyrinth of conflicts, or else they have already succeeded in seizing control and in reducing the ego to impotence. The growing number of people who have lost their relation to the Self provides a shattering object lesson as to where such a separation may lead.

"By his care for the psyche of his patients Jung tries to understand the meaning of philosophical, religious, and metaphysical statements and their relation to life, in order to apply them in his psychotherapy," says Jung's colleague and namesake.[17] Thus theology becomes a discussion of the *imago Dei* in man, and "trinitarian thinking is fettered to the reality of this world".[18] The "fetter" of this world adds itself as the fourth to the metaphysical Trinity, thereby making it a quaternity.[19]

The quaternity, above all in the form of the square, is one of the oldest symbols besides the circle for wholeness and completeness, symbolizing the parts, qualities, and aspects of unity,[20] and it is therefore natural to regard it as a God-image, as a representation of the Self. By manifesting itself in the psychic substance of man, the trinitarian divinity acquires a "body" and no longer pertains to the abstract, metaphysical world but to the physical world of concrete reality. Through the inclusion of this fourth dimension the extreme psychic opposites are combined in the Self and united in a paradoxical unity. "The self," says Jung, "is absolutely paradoxical in that it represents in every sense thesis and antithesis, and at the same time synthesis." [21] However, "only the paradox comes anywhere near to comprehending the fullness of life. Non-ambiguity and non-contraction are one-sided and thus unsuited to express the incomprehensible." [22]

Actually the Self is everywhere and behind everything. It is as though, all his life, man were circling round it, ever drawing closer in narrower and narrower circles, perceiving its effects and its actuality ever more clearly, but without ever unveiling its ultimate secret. "We are all in God's hands" is a saying that is often on men's lips, though they do not reflect that it also expresses their total abandonment to an unpredictable fate. Summing up what people have to say about their experience of wholeness, Jung puts it like this: "They came to themselves, they could accept themselves, they were able to become reconciled to themselves, and thus were reconciled to adverse circumstances and events. This is almost like what used to be expressed by saying: He has made his peace with God, he has sacrificed his own will, he has submitted himself to the will of God." [23] The right relation between ego and Self conveys something of this attitude of humility. For through the Self there speaks an authority which, as God's representative, has the character of fate. That is why the union of the ego with the Self is indistinguishable from a *unio mystica* with God, and is a shattering and profoundly religious experience.

An encounter with the Self is ecstatic because it gives man the experience of a trans-subjective reality that bursts the bounds of his ego. But therein lies its danger. The union of the ego with a suprapersonal, numinous power like the archetype of the Self means an expansion of personality which, if the ego does not immediately return to its place, leads to inflation, to a loss of the ego, and in the worst case to a psychosis. "The great psychic danger which is always connected with individuation, or the development of the self, lies in the identification of ego-consciousness with the self. This produces an inflation which threatens consciousness with dissolution . . . We have before our eyes as a warning just such a pair of friends distorted by inflation—Nietzsche and Zarathustra—but the warning has not been heeded. And what are we to make of Faust and Mephistopheles? The Faustian hybris is already the first step towards madness." [24] To linger in a *unio mystica,* as it were "egoless", is the supreme goal of Buddhist meditation, equivalent to "entering into *nirvana*", but, because it means the loss of an ever-renewed dialectical discussion between the ego and Self, it does *not,* according to Jung, correspond to the way of individuation for Western man.

The "ultimately unknowable", as Jung has called the Self, manifests itself at all stages of the individuation process, from birth to death, in specific symbols which, however varied, always reflect the state and attitude of the conscious mind. As a rule they manifest themselves when the ego has run into a cul-de-sac, when consciousness is confused and needs the guidance of a transpersonal authority, whether in youth or age. With the appearance of a Self-symbol the balance between the ego and the unconscious background can be restored. To be cut off from the helpful source of the Self always means isolation for the ego and loss of security. For this reason it is essential for psychic health—above all in maturer years—to keep the ego-Self axis unbroken and in constant dynamic mobility. Special methods used for this purpose in an analytically assisted individuation process, such as "active imagination" [25] in its various forms—writing, painting, sculpting, modelling, dancing, etc.—help to activate the psychic depths, to maintain the vital contact between conscious and unconscious contents, and to express the emerging symbols in plastic form.

In the course of these "imaginations", as also in dreams and fantasies, the "uniting symbols" will appear. These are the symbols that most vividly represent the fundamental order of the psyche, the union of its polaristic qualities. The most important among them are the *mandalas*.[26] They are the prime symbols of the Self, of psychic wholeness; Jung calls them "atomic nuclei" [27] of the psyche. They belong to the oldest religious symbols and are to be met with even in palaeolithic times. We find them in all cultures and among all peoples, but more particularly in the sphere of Buddhism, where the most artistically beautiful and most impressive examples may be found. Their commonest form is the circle or square, but many of them take the form of a flower, a cross, or a wheel, with a distinct inclination towards a quadratic structure. The peculiar symbolism of the mandala shows almost universally the same regularity, expressed in typical, symmetrical arrangement of its elements, these being always related to the centre. These structures not only express order, they also create order. Consequently, in the East, meditation on them is traditionally said to bring about an inner, psychic balance with healing powers.

If mandalas occur in dreams, it always means that there is a latent possibility of order. But if "disturbed mandalas" are produced—mandalas that are asymmetrical or disorganized in some way—this may be taken as a symptom of the momentary incapacity of the unconscious psyche to create order and achieve a state of balance. In other words, the self-regulating and self-curing powers of the psyche are disturbed.[28]

Apart from mandalas, other symbols of the Self are the sphere, the pearl, the diamond, crystal, flower, child, chalice, Anthropos, hermaphrodite, etc. It depends on the position of an object or figure in the dream context whether it should be taken as a symbol of the Self or not. In accordance with the

high value laid on the Self, figures of great religious significance often occupy the centre of the picture, e.g., Christ with
the four evangelists or Buddha with his disciples.

Depending on the psychic disposition of the individual,
however, and the degree of development he has reached, everything in creation, great or small, sublime or ridiculous, concrete or abstract, can become a symbol of the Self and compel
the conscious mind to react to this directive centre. *"Mille
sunt nomina,"* it is said of the *lapis philosophorum,* the stone
of the wise, an alchemical symbol of the Self. The criterion for
symbols of the Self is their numinosity. This is their constant
characteristic, for they represent a *coincidentia oppositorum,* a
union of opposites, in particular of conscious and unconscious
contents, and thus transcend rational understanding. Through
this union they bridge the dissociated portions of the psyche by
creating a *tertium,* a "third" thing, supraordinate to both
sides. Thus, for example, in alchemical symbolism this union is
represented as the royal brother and sister pair, i.e., as a union
of opposites, from whom the "divine child", the symbol of
unity, of the Self, is born. All these symbols are the vehicles
and at the same time the product of the "transcendent function",[29] that is, of the psyche's symbol-making capacity, of its
creative power.

Fateful as the confrontation with the Self may be, it is no
substitute for the trials of patience which the individual has
to go through during the stages of the individuation process,
any more than is the production of mandalas however numerous and of visions however ecstatic, as many people seem to
think. "Everything good is costly," says Jung, "and the development of personality is one of the most costly of all things. It
is a matter of saying yea to oneself, of taking oneself as the
most serious of tasks, of being conscious of everything one does,
and keeping it constantly before one's eyes in all its dubious
aspects—truly a task that taxes us to the utmost."[30] Patience is
its main postulate, for one must learn to "let things happen in
the psyche" without the continual interference and correction
of consciousness.

The Archetype of
the Individuation Process

THE individuation process, as a universal law of life, exhibits an archetypal pattern which remains more or less constant and regular. The signposts and milestones on the way are specific archetypal contents and motifs whose sequence cannot, however, be determined in advance and whose manifestations vary from individual to individual. The personal equation is also decisive for their understanding and assimilation. For "the method is merely the path, the direction taken by a man; the way he acts is the true expression of his nature." [1]

The symbolism of birth, life, death, and rebirth is part of the pattern of the individuation process. From the remotest times man has tried to express it in the imagery of myths and fairytales, in rituals and works of art, to capture the archetypal events in forms that are valid for all men.

Most of these myths and rituals have a phylogenetic, i.e., collectively valid, aspect as well as an ontogenetic one relating to the life-history of the individuals. [2] Many hero-myths, for instance, are a paradigm not only of the way of individuation of a single individual, but also of the evolution of consciousness in the course of history. The mythological fate of the hero, who was often a "sun-hero", symbolizing the rising and setting of the sun, may be regarded as a parallel of the archetypal development of the ego or consciousness of a single individual as well as of a group-consciousness. The evening, the sinking into the darkness of night, was the "death" of the sun; its rising in the morning, renewed, its "rebirth". For every rebirth is preceded by a death.

The fact that men speak of rebirth at all, that there has always been such a concept, allows us to infer that "a store of psychic experiences designated by that term must actually exist",[3] although not directly perceivable by the senses. This store of experience is a psychic reality substantiated by a consensus of opinion among all peoples at all epochs. "Rebirth is an affirmation that must be counted among the primordial affirmations of mankind."[4] It is not, however, always used in the same sense.[5] In the present context it means psychic rebirth within the lifetime of the individual, a renewal of personality in the sense of its growing completion, its tendency towards wholeness. Consequently, there can be a rebirth of the suppressed, unlived "nature" in man, as well as a rebirth of the neglected and undeveloped "spirit",[6] both of which must be sought in order to round out the individual into a whole.[7] But it will always be a "spiritual work" in so far as the co-operation of consciousness is the indispensable condition for both. Also, for most Westerners renewal in the sense of the Christian ideal will mean reaching a higher spiritual level, a casting off of the fetters of a technicized world.

Even so, rebirth can only proceed step by step, affecting the individual first in one part and then in another, until it finally encompasses his whole life. That is to say, the great arc of life whose ultimate aim is the rebirth of the whole personality will consist of many little "rebirth moments" and "rebirth events". Rebirth is not confined only to the analytically assisted individuation process, it relates also to the "natural" one. For every rebirth is an essential change, a transformation, and the possibility of this is inherent in all living organisms. It must be noted, however, that not every transformation is a process of individuation, though every individuation process consists of a chain of transformations. Transformation and individuation are closely connected but are by no means identical. Equally, it must be emphasized that transformation does not necessarily mean development. A transformation is usually a sudden occurrence; it can point in all sorts of different directions. But as a renewal or rebirth is always of its essence, transformation is an integral component of the individuation process, which in turn follows a line of development whose goal is psychic totality.

In the individuation process, as understood by Jung, the primary concern is the individual experience of "death and rebirth" through struggle and suffering, through a conscious, lifelong, unremitting endeavour to broaden the scope of one's consciousness and so attain a greater inner freedom. As well as going this personal way, the individual may also be transformed by taking part in or witnessing a collective rite or ceremony, but without the active participation of consciousness. Jung calls this "indirect rebirth".[8] The common factor here with the individuation process is the "transformation", but this does not represent a process of development though it may help to bring it about.

Such experiences can be observed primarily in religious ceremonies among primitive tribes, but they also occur in the more highly differentiated religions. In the latter the transformation seldom goes very deep; its effect usually does not last long because it is not consciously worked through. Nevertheless it can leave behind traces which serve to stimulate a further striving for psychic development, as also happens in the natural individuation process. Yet it must be admitted that in these situations there can be experiences, such as sudden conversions or illuminations, which affect the whole further course of life. The Christian Mass is in a sense an exception, in that both kinds of transformation can occur in it. For one who participates in it only as a collective being it remains a possibility of transformation that belongs to the second category; but if the participant consciously devotes himself as an individual being to becoming one with Christ in the communion, he is drawn into a progressive psychic development which leads to rebirth on a higher level, thus approximating to the way of individuation as understood by Jung.

Both kinds of individuation process, in their various forms, can be found in numerous myths and legends which offer more or less apt analogies to the way of individuation. In the "natural" individuation process, which runs on without the intervention of consciousness, as well as in the "methodically guided" one, which is consciously worked through, a wealth of more or less striking parallels can be adduced with the symbolism of mythology. In the myths which have the daily course of the sun for their theme, whether it be Jonah in the whale, Herakles in the sun-vessel,[9] the Egyptian goddess Nut, who devours the sun every evening and gives birth to it every morning,[10] the natural individuation process is depicted symbolically in its eternal cyclic recurrence, as manifested in the alternation of day and night, in the succession of the seasons, in the rising and passing of the generations, etc.[11] Here, as in all unconscious processes, there is succession and recurrence without any lasting transformation; the process is bound to the laws of nature. Unlike the consciously experienced individuation process it is not an *opus contra naturam*, except in the special case of an active life courageously lived and consciously shaped.[12] Whenever our consciousness intervenes and takes an active part, renewal and differentiation will follow. Probably every process of psychic development in individuals with a relatively unconsolidated ego is subject only to a "natural" individuation. Yet the possibility of conscious transformation, of being reborn again and again until full psychic development is reached, seems to be laid by fate on those who already bear in themselves a brighter light of consciousness, and this light will gain in strength and splendour as a result of their psychic transformation and renewal.

Not only the two forms of individuation, the "natural" and the "methodically assisted", but also its two main phases, that

of the first and that of the second half of life,[13] have their mythological analogies. Sometimes only the first phase, sometimes
the second, and sometimes both are symbolically represented.
Although the whole process plots the course of conscious realization, the first phase aims at the crystallization of a stable ego,
and the second at the achievement of a permanent relationship
between the ego and the Self.[14] Accordingly, each phase is characterized by a more or less marked variation of the archetypal
ground-pattern.

Most of the creation-myths, too, when looked at psychologically, can be understood as symbolical representations of the
original coming of consciousness, as its birth, so to speak,
which happens for the first time in the psyche of the newborn
child. When, for instance, in the Babylonian creation-myth, to
name but one of many, the hero Marduk, who stands for the
sun, kills and dismembers with his sword, symbolizing the
sun's rays, the dragon Tiamat, the embodiment of chaos and
the primal darkness, and the world arises from the parts of its
body,[15] this is an analogy of the creation of the world and the
coming of consciousness. The sword of light is plunged into the
darkness of unconsciousness, the darkness is dispelled, and objects take shape. They are "born", to so speak, they can now be
seen, discriminated, and named, they are perceived and appre-
hended by consciousness. This creation of the world as the
coming of consciousness is an event that is ceaselessly repeated
in the life of man. Every time it happens a little bit of new
territory, of new knowledge, a newly won insight, is added to
the field of consciousness, which is "reborn" in more comprehensive form both in the natural and in the analytically assisted individuation process.

The central content of the numerous myths in which a
dragon or some other monster is dismembered is the acquisition of an independent ego-personality, for which purpose the
"devouring, terrible mother" must be overcome. If the individual is to develop and consolidate his ego, the "mother" as
the symbol of the darkness of unconsciousness must first be de-

stroyed by the bright light of youthful consciousness, symbolized by the sun's rays or by the arrow, sword, or club. In the second phase of the individuation process it is no longer a question of destruction but of a descent into the dark realm of the unconscious, symbolized by the devouring maw of the death-dealing monster. There in the depths, in the creative womb of the "mother", and with the help of the strong light of consciousness, is found the "treasure hard to attain", "the precious hoard"—designations for the Self—which the hero must bring back to the light of day. This journey to the underworld, the so-called *nekyia*,[16] is the model on which most of these myths and fates are based. We find it as the descent into hell in the life of Christ, preceding his resurrection. The creation of the world through the dismemberment of the maternal dragon is therefore the archetypal ground-pattern for the task of the first phase of individuation; being devoured by it, to emerge matured, transformed, and reunited with the Self, is the mark of the second.

The numerous puberty rites still extant among primitives today present useful analogies of this first phase, though with certain limitations. In contrast to an individuation process extending over the whole span of life, these rites occur in a compressed form and only during a fixed period, and are an event in which the neophytes participate collectively. The underlying ideas and aims are nevertheless similar to those of the individuation process, and are often actually identical. We find in these rites images and motifs which offer astounding analogies with those of the first phase and even with those of the second. All of them are concerned with a psychic renewal of the individual, with a rebirth characteristic of the individuation process.

Let us take as an example the initiation rites[17] which the young men (as well as the girls) have to go through in order to be accepted as full members of the tribe, and to marry and found a family. Here we shall speak only of the rites for the men and their "initiation into outer reality", into adulthood.[18]

The life of primitives still bears a strong biological stamp. Once a man's biological life has started to decline, his role is over and done with, so to speak. For this reason the second phase of the individuation process, spiritual transformation and differentiation, or "initiation into inner reality", is reserved only for the few, namely the medicine-men. They are the wise men of the tribe, their dignity and rich experience make them the "seers" among their fellow tribesmen. They are the exceptions, who in their youth underwent the trials of initiation with the others, yet in their striving for further development were able to gain deeper insights, judgment, and shrewdness in human affairs, by virtue of which they possess healing power and occupy a leading position in the tribe.[19]

In most tribes the initiation rites the young men have to go through are, with small variations, based on the same or a similar archetypal ground-pattern. They represent rebirth ceremonies, that is, the rebirth of the child into manhood, which can take place only if the child is rigorously separated from his previous life and begins a new one.

The most important stages of these rites therefore consist in the strict segregation of the neophytes from their previous environment, from women and most of all from their mothers. They are secluded for months, sometimes for years, in some remote spot, where they are initiated by the medicine-man into the secrets of the tribe, into the world of the ancestor spirits, circumcised, instructed about sex and prepared for marriage. They learn what an adult needs to do in life—hunting, fishing, building, handiwork of all kinds. Finally they emerge from their seclusion, often naked as babes, and are taught how to eat, walk, and talk as though they had just been born. They are given new clothes and often new names.[20]

Sometimes they are secluded in a hut shaped like the mouth of a huge dragon or crocodile,[21] symbolizing the devouring aspect of the mother from which they have to free themselves. In some tribes, as a test of their intrepidity and strength of will, the neophytes have to step over the body of the mother, lying in the doorway, or even tread on her belly without batting an eyelid.

Living in such a "dragon house" can be equated with the "descent into hell", with a symbolic death, which is an essential part of the initiation and a prelude to rebirth.[22] It is a radical psychic upheaval for the sake of producing a new attitude to life, of establishing relations with the mysterious powers of the Beyond, the ancestors, who are charged with "mana", i.e., possess the most efficacious powers. In Jungian terms, this would mean establishing relations with the numinous powers of the collective unconscious, the archetypes, which dwell in the psychic background of all members of the tribe. In the case of the single individual, it would mean the realization of a relation to the Self. In this way, perhaps owing to the relative shortness of the primitive's life, the most important step in the second phase of individuation is anticipated.

Akin to these more or less primitive initiation ceremonies, which still take place on the bodily plane, are the rites for initiating adults into various mysteries, secret societies, and cults. Though they too are often confined to a certain period, they have more the character of an "initiation into inner reality"; their content is related more to the second phase of the individuation process. In this connection we might mention— to name but a few—the Isis and Demeter mysteries of antiquity,[23] those of the Orphics, the Adonis cults,[24] and the initiation ceremonies of the Freemasons[25] and Rosicrucians.[26] Various forms of initiation have always existed, and still exist, among practically all peoples, for the longing for psychic development and wholeness, for contact with the divine in some form, is an archetypal datum and has always found expression in rites and cults of all kinds. But in spite of thorough ethnological researches, and investigations into the history of religion, the description of such initiations is always conjectural, because strict silence about what they experience is almost al-

ways imposed on the initiates. Moreover it is of the essence of
the mystery that it can never be fully explained or fathomed.
There is ample evidence that initiation rites of this kind also
found their way into Christianity.[27] In a certain sense baptism,
and above all the Mass, can be understood as rebirth mysteries,[28] since their purpose is a transformation and renewal of
the personality. They are integral components of the individuation process.

In his writings, Jung has devoted less attention to the first
phase of individuation than to the second. On this he lays special weight, as it is the most neglected phase of psychic development. Calling it the simplest ground-plan, the archetypal
ground-pattern or symbolic model for the individual's way of
individuation, Jung has on various occasions referred to the
myth of the "night sea journey" [29] cited by Frobenius, which he
named the "whale dragon myth".[30] The schematic representation[31] of this journey, which occurs in numerous variations, is
valid for the individuation process as a whole as well as for
each of its stages:

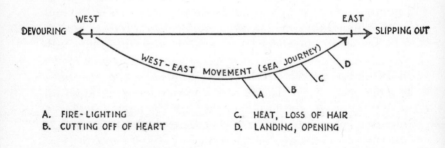

A. FIRE-LIGHTING
B. CUTTING OFF OF HEART

C. HEAT, LOSS OF HAIR
D. LANDING, OPENING

The accompanying text runs:
"A hero is devoured by a water-monster in the West (*devouring*). The animal travels with him to the East (*sea journey*). Meanwhile, the hero lights a fire in the belly of the monster (*fire-lighting*), and feeling hungry, cuts himself a piece of
the heart (*cutting off of heart*). Soon afterwards, he notices
that the fish has glided on to dry land (*landing*); he immedi-

ately begins to cut open the animal from within (*opening*); then he slips out (*slipping out*). It was so hot in the fish's belly that all his hair has fallen out (*heat, loss of hair*). The hero may at the same time free all those who were previously devoured by the monster, and who now slip out too."

The hero stands for the sun (i.e., for ego-consciousness), the fish's belly for the underworld (realm of the unconscious), for the night through which the sun makes its journey. It sinks in the West, rises again in the East. The lighting of a fire in the darkness can be interpreted as a sudden flickering up of the light of consciousness, which enables the hero to find the "essence" (heart), the supreme value hidden in the darkness. By eating it he discovers the "meaning" of the night sea journey and has thereby prepared the way for his deliverance. For as soon as consciousness pierces the darkness, it begins to approach full luminosity: the fish glides slowly on to dry land, into a conscious world. As a result of the "heat", i.e., the emotions that shook the hero in his prison, he is "initiated" into the mysteries of the darkness, and becomes humble and wise. He loses his original power of thought (loss of hair) and, on cutting his way out ("rebirth"), emerges bald as a newborn babe. Through the "slipping out" of the sun many other contents that were hidden in the darkness come to light and can be perceived.

This schema is valid for every phase of conscious realization, e.g., for that daily journey of our consciousness through the night, during sleep. As in the story of Jonah, it remains an open question whether the water-monster dies or goes on living after the hero slips out. Presumably both variants occur. In the first case it would mean the permanent survival of the victorious hero, after the model of a "methodical" individuation; in the second it would be a cyclic occurrence, as the sun, i.e., the hero, could always be devoured again so long as the monster lives.

Entry into the belly of the monster, i.e., the submersion of consciousness in the darkness of the unconscious, can be regarded as a return to the mother's womb, as a regression. This should not be looked upon as an incestuous wish-fulfilment, as Freud thought, but as the possibility of rebirth. It is not something negative only, but in Jung's prospective interpretation also a necessary and positive event. The realm of the unconscious is not merely a deadly maw and certainly not a refuse bin; it is a treasure-house of the nourishing and creative forces which dwell in all living things. When brought into contact with consciousness, they become activated and place themselves at its disposal: they are "reborn".[32]

The fact that Jung often used the "night sea journey" as a model for the individuation process even in the first half of life has repeatedly given rise to misunderstandings. Because individuation extends through the whole of life, many people overlooked the fact that its first half stands under a different sign from the second and therefore expresses itself in different symbols. They assumed that only a person in the second half of life can individuate, and they regarded the process always as an analogy of the "descent into the underworld". But on closer examination this model is to some extent applicable to all stages of the process of individuation. It can be said with some justification that every act of conscious realization is a plunging into the darkness of the underworld and a re-emergence from it, such as we experience every day in our sleep and dreams, and that the "night sea journey" therefore retains its validity for every kind of "rebirth", i.e., conscious realization, whether it belong to the first or to the second phase of individuation. Even so we must, if we wish to reduce the archetypal material to some kind of order, try to distinguish in principle between its two specific forms.

If we examine the material in which the two main phases of the individuation process are symbolized, we find them most clearly represented in most of the classical mythologems. Let us take a look at the Egyptian myth of Osiris, for instance.[33] There the dividing line between the first and the second phase occurs when the sun-god Osiris stands at the height of his earthly power and has accomplished all the tasks demanded by the first half of life by winning his place in the world and begetting his son Horus as his successor. At that point he falls a victim to his evil counterpart, his brother Set, is dismembered, and begins his journey to the underworld in a coffer. He enters into the womb of the mother, symbolized by the coffer, the sea, and the tree-coffin, and, after his sister-wife Isis has sought the fourteen parts of his body and put them together again, he is reborn and appears anew in his son Harpocrates, the "weak in the legs". This son was begotten in the underworld, the realm of the dead, and has no fixed abode in the real world but, instead, is initiated into the mysteries. This may be taken as an indication that the biological power of procreation, which pertains to the first half of life and whose fruit is the "fleshly" child Horus, is superseded in the second by a symbolic, spiritual one which brings the "spiritual" child to birth. This spiritual procreative power is symbolized by the substitute phallus which was made by Isis and put in the place of the phallus that was lost during the dismemberment and could not be found again.[34]

Although in the individuation process, aiming as it does at psychic totality, the "missing" element must always be sought and integrated, and spirit and nature, the heavenly and the chthonic realm, be considered in equal measure, it is nevertheless the normal pattern of life that the biological should occupy the foreground in youth and the spiritual in maturer years. Consequently most of the myths paralleling the individuation process culminate in an anchoring in inner reality, in the spiritual realm. Even in the "hero-myths", such as that of Theseus, which may likewise be cited as analogies, the overcoming of mortal dangers leads in the end to a victory over the agents of darkness and to a rebirth in regenerated form.

As a further example we may cite Tantra yoga,[35] where again the aim is ultimate spiritualization. It too must be regarded as a way of initiation, with a course of development that culmi-

nates in the acquisition of an illuminated consciousness, of a
higher level of being. In this system the *kundalini* serpent,
symbolizing the stream of libido or psychic energy, rises up
through six *chakras,* or psychic centres, beginning with the one
in the perineal region, to the highest *chakra,* situated in the
crown of the head, where consciousness unites with Atman,
the divine, thus bringing about illumination. The first three
chakras, the centres of the instinctual region in man, reach up
as far as the diaphragm; the other three, situated higher,
spread their energy through the spiritual regions of the body.
The dividing line is thus between the navel and the heart,
where the world of instinct "ends", so to speak; this instinctual
region is correlated with the phase of life in which the main
tasks demanded by these centres are accomplished. From there
the *kundalini* serpent strives ever upward, to the head, to the
centres of the higher forms of being; this corresponds to the
striving in the second half of life for spiritual values. This one-
sided striving only in an upward direction reflects the religious
world-view of Tantra yoga, for which the supreme goal is the
dissolution of the ego and the vivification and sovereignty of
Atman.[36] It contrasts strongly with Jung's view, according to
which the consolidation of the ego is the indispensable condition for any "higher consciousness"; but by "higher consciousness" he understands something different from the Hindu,
namely, a psychological process. For the Hindu, on the other
hand, it has a metaphysical rather than a psychological character. Nevertheless the common factor in yoga exercises, which
permits a certain analogy with the individuation process, is the
striving for a renewal of the personality through a series of
related ideas and experiences such as are found in many rites
of initiation, and above all the fact that it is always an individual transformation occurring outside the collective.

Likewise related to the individuation process only in their
ground-pattern, but different in form and expression, are the
spiritual exercises of Ignatius of Loyola, which subject the individual to a psychic process that is supposed to purify and

regenerate his personality. The immediate aim of these exercises is to produce a profound psychic transformation which should have a lasting effect on a man's whole being. In their original form they were undertaken only once in a lifetime and were concentrated into four weeks. Today they are carried out in one-week exercises repeated every year so as to maintain the efficacy of the transformation. They begin with a self-observation and self-reflection which help the practitioner to become fully conscious of his sins, and then go on to demand a personal, conscious way of living and a decision affecting his attitude to the world, which has to be directed towards Christ as the central point and exemplar. As the final foundation and confirmation of this decision, the stations of the way leading from the passion of Christ to his resurrection have to be followed concretely, so to speak, in an inner vision and actively experienced. Psychologically interpreted, this last part of the exercises can in a sense be understood as corresponding to the second phase of the individuation process, as a journey through the underworld of suffering, through a mystic, symbolic death into a kind of rebirth. The first part of the exercises would correspond to the consolidation of the ego through the realization of one's shadow and thus is characterized by the necessity for a free decision.[37]

One other Catholic rite may perhaps be adduced as a further analogy; this is the Blessing of the Paschal Candle, celebrated in the Easter liturgy on the night of Holy Saturday as a preparation for Christ's resurrection on Easter Sunday. It is performed during the last six hours of Holy Saturday and, psychologically considered, represents in compressed, symbolic form the birth, death, and rebirth of the human soul. Its main features are as follows: In the porch of the unlit church, fire is struck from a flint and with it a giant candle is lighted, representing Christ, the Light. Solemnly, this candle is carried into the darkened church by the celebrating priest, surrounded by four other candles, symbols of the four evangelists. On the way to the altar all the little candles, which the members of the congregation hold in their hands, are lighted at the flame of the Christ candle, as a symbol that every mortal has received an immortal spark from the eternal light of the Lord. Then the story of the Creation is recited and a solemn ceremony of baptism[38] performed before the altar, through which the congregation, as though representing the whole collective, partakes of a new baptism. At the end Christ's passion and resurrection are celebrated in a Mass and the sacrament is administered to all present, making them one with Christ. For through the communion the Christian has a share in the body and blood of Christ, whose fate repeats itself in him.

From this mystery we may derive the following psychological interpretation. The candles shining in the dark church, i.e., in the realm of the unconscious, receive their luminosity from the one candle, the symbol of the Self, and, through the baptism, each is endowed with its unique psychic reality. This corresponds in some degree with the development of the ego in the first phase of individuation, the journey through suffering and danger into the grace of rebirth, which finds its symbolic expression in the Mass and in the resultant transformation.

Finally we must say a few words about the endeavours of the alchemists,[39] who projected the psychic transformation process into the transmutation of metals, and experienced it as the transformation of matter. The parallels with the "methodical" process of individuation are so astonishing that they compelled Jung to undertake a thorough investigation of these pre-scientific practices. He established that in the alchemical treatises, with their often bizarre symbolism, there is hidden a "Hermetic philosophy", a kind of secret doctrine which formulated the methods for achieving psychic wholeness, a psychic transformation akin to the individuation process.[40]

The alchemical *opus* starts with the conception of a primary matter, the *prima materia,* which was sought in lead, and, following the principle of *solve et coagula* ("dissolve and coagulate")—in psychological terms: separate and combine the material of the conscious and unconscious—proceeds by stages (usually four, eight, or twelve) to the production of the *lapis philosophorum,* symbolizing the Self. The turning-point from the first to the second phase of individuation can be localized between the third and fourth stages of the alchemical transformation. This is where the confrontation with the shadow, represented by the state of blackness or *nigredo,* takes place, after the division of the *prima materia* into four parts, which permits a discrimination and differentiation of its contents. Here, if everything goes well, the typologically dominant function is differentiated [41] and the shadow to a large extent integrated, which corresponds to the crystallization of the ego. This is followed by a second *nigredo* stage, a descent of the ego into the underworld, a "killing" (*mortificatio*) and a "decay" (*putrefactio*) of the material, which can be taken as an analogy of the dismemberment of Osiris and his enclosure in the coffin. If this stage persists, it can manifest itself as a psychosis. The process is not yet completed, however. After the "death" the reascent begins: anima and animus qualities are made conscious,[42] a *destillatio* or purification follows, in which what was originally one is again divided and reunited so that a *coagulatio* can take place, analogous on the psychological level to the confrontation with the archetypal figures, the mana-personalities.[43]

The *opus* ends, ideally, with the transmutation of lead into gold, the noblest metal, or, in the language of the alchemists, with the birth of *filius philosophorum,* or stone of the wise, the *lapis*[44] which was supposed to be incorruptible and eternal. In psychological terms: the encounter with the Self and the conscious possession of the Self can give man a feeling of lasting security through the relation he has found to the God-image. This state may well be compared with the "hardness" of the stone,[45] though it would be a mistake to suppose that the possession of this "stone" spares a man all further difficulties for ever. What it vouchsafes is above all the experience that this relationship is indestructible for the ego, because it accords with man's own nature and can always be re-established in time of danger.

The fact that the individuation process with its two great phases can also leave a symbolic deposit in the psyche of a contemporary is illustrated by the dream of a thirty-eight-year-old married woman. She dreamt it shortly after having met Jung for the first time—socially, not professionally. She had no notion of psychology, let alone of Jung's depth psychology, and no knowledge of even the most elementary psychological concepts, nor had she ever been interested in them. Neither had she ever dealt with dreams, so that the dream, which shook her to the depths, found her quite unprepared, unarmed by any foreknowledge, and yet it seemed to point the way.

The action of the dream took place at first in the bay of a beautiful Baroque castle, in a high room with twelve corners, the walls and ceiling of which were covered with mirrors. The room was completely empty. The dreamer was lying fully dressed on the smooth parquet floor, which, like a *trottoir roulant,* revolved round a finely chased metal knob to which she held fast with her hands. Seeing herself reflected on all sides as well as from above threw her into the greatest confusion; distorted, chopped into pieces, she could hardly recognize herself. To begin with the floor moved quite slowly, then it got faster and faster until it spun round like mad and made her completely dizzy. Her clothes fell away from her, and she was seized with a terrible fear that she might not be able to hold on to the knob and would be flung by the centrifugal force of the movement into the wall mirrors, where she might be fatally wounded. In vain she tried to slow it down, in vain she tried to hang on. Helpless, naked, and terrified she finally crashed against the wall, which shattered into a thousand pieces and seemed to engulf her. Then the room and castle vanished.

Still alive, but bleeding from a thousand wounds, the dreamer now lay out of doors, naked on her back, in a freshly ploughed field. All round was silence. A pallid February sun lit the scene, nearing the zenith. On her left side sat a man, the man she loved, dressed in a long white shirt, weeping. His tears wetted the shirt. With the wet patches he gently wiped the dreamer's wounds until they closed up, healed. Thankfully she looked up at him and up at the sky. Suddenly she felt the earth beginning to move beneath her, as though it were growing together with her back. At the same time she felt that the man was no longer at her side, but was stretched out on top of her, motionless and weighing a ton. The weight pressed her deeper and deeper down, but the earth seemed to go on thrusting and pushed her upwards. As it continued to push, the piled-up mounds of earth began to sprout. Grass shot up in the air, the field became a verdant meadow, and the dreamer became one with it. She herself was the earth, was blossoming nature. But the man who lay on top of her grew lighter and lighter as she grew together with the earth. Soon he seemed to have melted into air, he became the firmament arching above the meadow. Thus they celebrated the marriage of heaven and earth, the union of the masculine and feminine principles.

In the first part of this extraordinary dream one can see the first phase of the individuation process represented. It shows how the ego of the dreamer became endangered by her extremely extraverted life, symbolized by the revolving parquet floor. Her life, played out before the mirrors of the surrounding world, gets distorted and refracted. Driven to extremes, all defences fall away from her, she has to experience her naked reality—and be shattered. This is at the same time the acid test of the ego, which has to be exposed to all dangers and yet survive them. Only then will it be strong enough to confront the world of the archetypes in the second half of life, that is, in the second phase of individuation. Freed from the fetters of her previous life, healed of her wounds by the man who loves her, the dreamer can now be wholly woman and seek to solve the problem of relating to the other sex. She can now recognize him as the archetypal image of the spirit, and herself as the archetypal image of the nourishing earth. From the entanglements of a personal tie, in which she felt the man as a heavy weight, there is formed, through her oneness with nature, an archetypal relationship, an ecstatic union of opposites in a unitary mode of being. The animus, the masculine element in her, is no longer the other person, the man, but a spirit belonging to her and united with her, whose symbol is heaven. In this dream the way of individuation the dreamer has to follow is prefigured in a powerful symbolic event. Such a dream works on one like a task; it points the way to one's destiny.

The profound longing for initiation, i.e., for a share in a regenerated, more perfect mode of being, is embedded in the soul of man from the very beginning. Initiation rites and their motifs thread the history of symbolism and accompany life from its beginning to its end. The symbolic world of fairytales, rich in wonders, is studded with initiations. In this wonder-world the hero and heroine pass through trials and perils, risking their lives to be delivered from a curse, to obtain the precious jewel of the Self, to begin a new life, better and more complete. Children, grown-ups, and greybeards are all equally fascinated by the magic which fairytales spread around them.

The symbolism of the individuation process has often been elaborated in world literature. Classic examples are Dante's *Divine Comedy* and Goethe's *Faust*. Psychological interpretations of the symbolism in the Jungian sense may be found in the writings of Linda Fierz-David,[46] Esther Harding,[47] and Cornelia Brunner,[48] to name but a few.

Initiation motifs and ideas related to, and even identical with, those occurring in the individuation process have from earliest times found their way into all cultures, often in the form of beautifully elaborate rites and ceremonies, often only as fragments. Even though they cannot be carried over into concrete reality, and are thrust into the background by the hectic, technicized life of our time, they still go on living, at least in the realm of the unconscious psyche; from there they rise up again and take shape in dreams, fantasies, and works of art. Just as a quite simple tune, consisting of only a few notes, can be preserved as a ground-pattern in all kinds of variations, marches, fugues, symphonies, etc., and can always be found again, so initiation, i.e., individuation—the great arc of birth, life, death, and rebirth—is present in a thousand manifestations as a model and represents in its most primitive as well as its most complex forms an eternal possibility of new human experience and development.

If we attempt to enumerate the various aspects of the individuation process, we find that they can be summed up under the following groups, though the individual groups will tend to overlap:

1. a) the "natural" process which is the ordinary course of human life
   b) the "methodically" or "analytically assisted" process worked out by Jung
2. a) a process experienced and worked out as an "individual way"
   b) an initiation resulting from participation in a collective event
3. a) a gradual development consisting of many little transformations
   b) a sudden transformation brought about by a shattering experience
4. a) a continuous development extending over the whole life-span
   b) a cyclic process constantly recurring in unchanged form
5. a) a process in which only the first phase is accomplished
   b) a process in which both phases follow in sequence
6. a) a process prematurely interrupted by outer or inner circumstances
   b) an undeveloped process remaining in atrophied form
   c) a "sick" or "defective" process

This list with its groupings should not, of course, be understood in any dogmatic sense. Its purpose is merely to facilitate a survey of the different points of view from which the individuation process can be observed, and it applies to both forms, the "natural" as well as the "methodically" or "analytically" assisted" course of development.

Analogies with the individuation process could be multiplied without end, but here we will mention only a few of them. In his indefatigable researches into the whole history of symbolism Jung has put together and interpreted a mass of more or less pertinent analogies to the process as a whole or to its individual parts. He found them, however, above all in the dreams and fantasies of contemporary men and women,[49] with whose psychic troubles he was concerned as a psychotherapist. They indicated to him the need for broad-based comparative researches and led him to the observation and description of the individuation process in modern individuals, and of the possible ways of furthering it analytically. "My life has been permeated and held together by one idea and one goal: namely, to penetrate into the secret of the personality. Everything can be explained from this central point, and all my works relate to this one theme," says Jung.[50] In his immense life-work, more particularly in his *Two Essays on Analytical Psychology*,[51] his commentaries on *The Secret of the Golden Flower*[52] and *The Tibetan Book of the Dead*,[53] in *Psychology and Alchemy*,[54] "The Psychology of the Transference",[55] *Aion*,[56] and finally in his *Mysterium Coniunctionis*,[57] he has set down the results of his experiences and investigations, and, despite their difficulty, those dealing with alchemy deserve special attention.[58]

✓ Jung has constantly emphasized that he considers the individuation process as worked out by him, i.e., as a confrontation between the conscious and unconscious contents of the psyche, to be the way of development specially suited to present-day Western man. Mystery religions and initiation rites with similar forms and similar goals have existed at all times and places, but, Jung thinks, they should not be taken over uncritically by the West, because they spring from an alien spiritual and religious culture. Equally, people belonging to alien cultures can individuate only in the way that accords with their own natures. Jung's way of individuation will always remain foreign to them, just as in Jung's view a Westerner will never be able to practise yoga in its true spirit or become a yogi. Even though the archetypal "ground-plan" of the individuation process remains more or less constant, its expression varies according to environment, the spirit of the time, the religious attitude and conscious situation of each individual.

What a profound insight the Oriental sage possesses into this simple and self-evident truth was once brought home to me by a Sinologist, the late Erwin Rousselle. When a European, who had spent six years in a Japanese monastery in order to be initiated, left the place, he received as a farewell present from his guru a carefully wrapped package. He undid the wrappings and saw to his utmost astonishment that it was a magnificently bound Bible. In this way he was tactfully given to understand from what source he as a European could best obtain "initiation".

The Individual Way

PERSONALITY can never develop unless one chooses one's own way consciously and makes this an ethical decision. Not only is a causal motive needed, for instance an emergency of some kind, but a conscious decision must lend its force to the process of personality development. If the first is lacking, then the so-called development would be mere acrobatics of the will. And without conscious decision the development would remain a dull, unconscious automatism. One can, however, decide on one's own way only when one is convinced it is the only right one. Should any other way be considered better, then it would certainly be preferred to the development of one's own personality. But the other ways are conventions of a moral, social, political, philosophical, or religious nature.

It may seem astonishing that the decision to be oneself should have to be equated with an "ethical act", for it should be the most obvious thing in the world to develop one's personality and stand by one's peculiarities. But that is by no means so. All too many people do not live their own lives, and generally they know next to nothing about their real nature. They make convulsive efforts to "adapt", not to stand out in any way, to do exactly what the opinions, rules, regulations, and habits of the environment demand as being "right". They are slaves of "what people think", "what people do", etc. That this leads to false attitudes and, if the discrepancy between their real nature and their sham nature becomes too great, to neuroses hardly needs stressing. Of such people Schopenhauer rightly says: ". . . the sphere of what we are for other people is their consciousness, not ours; it is the kind of figure we make in their eyes, together with the thoughts which this arouses . . . people in the highest position in life, with all their brilliance, pomp, display, magnificence and general show, may well say: Our happiness lies entirely outside us, it exists only in the heads of others." [1]

The individuation process in the Jungian sense means the conscious realization and integration of all the possibilities congenitally present in the individual. It is opposed to any kind of conformity and, as a therapeutic factor in analytical work, also demands the rejection of those prefabricated psychic matrices in which most people would like to live. It shows that everyone can have his own direction, his mission, and it can make meaningful the lives of those people who suffer from the feeling that they are unable to come up to the collective norms and collective ideals. To those who are not recognized by the collective, who are rejected and even despised, it can restore their faith in themselves, give them back their human dignity, and assure them of their place in the world. "We could therefore translate individuation as 'coming to selfhood' or 'self-realization' ", for it means "becoming an 'in-dividual', and, in so far as 'individuality' embraces our innermost, last, and incomparable uniqueness, it also implies becoming one's own self." [2]

Individuation cannot be anything other than a unique and individual development, and it is questionable whether it allows of the acceptance of any norm. It brings a knowledge of the infinite capacity for development of the human psyche, and its mode of operation is enough in itself to put it outside the range of anything measurable. For the setting up of absolute standards by which an individuation process could be adjudged "right" or "wrong" would merely mean the acceptance of various patterns of ideals as a starting point and would come suspiciously close to the above-mentioned "prefabricated psychic matrices".

The fact, nevertheless, that conventions always flourish in some form proves that the overwhelming majority of men do not choose their own way but the way of convention, and develop something that is collectively valid at the cost of their own wholeness. This has its justification and also, no doubt, its good reasons. It is reserved only for the few to tread the thorny path of individuation, as envisaged by Jung, and to carry on the torch which—so we will hope—an increasing number of such individuals will follow.

Not only is the individual placed between the power of consciousness and that of his unconscious psyche, he is also a unique, unrepeatable being and at the same time a member of the collective and has to do justice to both. So far as an analytically assisted individuation process is concerned, no general rules can be laid down for dealing with this relationship. For on the one hand, it is said, man is a herd animal and reaches full health only as a social being, and on the other hand the very next case may invert this proposition and demonstrate that he is fully healthy only when he deviates from the norm and aims only at himself, that is, when he pursues his own individual way. For only as a "healthy" person can he live in accordance with his God-given task.

Jung attributes a key importance to the individual. According to him, only a change in the attitude of the individual can initiate a change in the psychology of nations. "The great events of world history are, at bottom, profoundly unimportant. In the last analysis, the essential thing is the life of the individual. This alone makes history, here alone do the great transformations first take place, and the whole future, the whole history of the world, ultimately springs as a gigantic summation from these hidden sources in individuals. In our most private and most subjective lives we are not only the passive witnesses of our age, and its sufferers, but also its makers." [3] And elsewhere: "Virtually everything depends on the human psyche and its functions. It should be worthy of all the attention we can give it, especially today, when everyone admits that the weal and woe of the future will be decided neither by the threat of wild animals, nor by natural catastrophes, nor by the danger of worldwide epidemics, but simply and solely by the psychic changes in man." [4]

Watching in alarm the steadily increasing, suction-like power of the State, the impotence of the individual in face of the power concentrated in the hands of so-called leaders, Jung observes: "We are all fascinated and overawed by statistical truths and large numbers and are daily apprised of the nullity and futility of the individual personality, since it is not represented and personified by any mass organization." [5]

It is a striking fact that the majority of men are merely "fragmentary personalities" and that anything like complete individuals form a great exception. Jung emphasizes, however, that "in order to undergo a far-reaching psychological development, neither outstanding intelligence nor any other talent is necessary, since in this development moral qualities can make up for intellectual shortcomings". [6] So far as every individual has the law of his life inborn in him, it is theoretically and in principle possible for everyone to follow that law and become a personality, to achieve relative wholeness, [7] which in the last resort is always the product of a life individually lived.

The idea that, in order to attain this wholeness, one must have experienced life in all its aspects proceeds from the generalization, applicable to the average member of society, that he must marry, have children, practise a profession, and so on, which amounts to leading a good bourgeois existence. But this would exclude all those whose lives deviate from the average and follow a law and pattern of their own, above all "exceptions" like many artists and men of genius, priests, nuns, unmarried persons, and the disabled, etc.

Although the ground-pattern, structure, phases, and stations of the individuation process may remain constant, its expres-

sion, the way the individual experiences it and is matured by
it, is unique and cannot be repeated. Naturally it seems—provisionally at least—not everyone's choice, but rather a quite
special fate, and to require a special summons or an inescapable inner impulse in order to undertake an analytically assisted individuation and persevere with it. "The individuation
process is, psychically, a borderline phenomenon which needs
special conditions in order to become conscious. Perhaps it is a
first step along a path of development to be trodden by the
men of the future—a path which, for the time being, has taken
a pathological turn and landed Europe in catastrophe." [8] Nevertheless the growing longing of man for a better understanding of himself and the world allows one to hope that he will
one day manage to cope more effectively with all the evil and
destructiveness that rise up out of the abysses of his soul.

Those who are not seized by this longing, but find safety and
security in the masses, will never be ready to follow consciously
the way of individuation, since to begin with it spells isolation
for the individual. It is as though he were a mountain whose
peak is the more isolated the higher it reaches; yet at its deeper
levels it shares the same earth with all other mountains. How
unpopular the individual way must be today, in an age of
conformism, of fitting into the collective, and of psychotherapeutic endeavours for "interpersonal relationship",[9] will be
clear to everyone. Especially in our automated Western world,
where there is less and less room for genuine feelings, man
seeks all the more desperately for security and hopes to find it
in the lap of the collective. He fears solitude, as it might force
him to think about himself.

We should not forget that every man, as well as having collective traits and being conditioned by the society to which he
belongs, is a unique combination of unique qualities. That is
why only a very few people are capable of putting themselves
into the psyche of another. Even the person we think we know
best is fundamentally a stranger to us, however much he may
affirm that he feels completely understood. At most we may
guess and feel our way into his otherness, but we can never

interpret or judge it and have to accept it with respect. "At bottom," says Jung, "all psychic events are so deeply grounded in the archetype and are so much interwoven with it that in every case considerable critical effort is needed to separate the unique from the typical with any certainty. Ultimately, every individual life is at the same time the eternal life of the species." [10] A striking example of this is the human fingerprint. Each one shows a pattern like a labyrinth, yet each is so different from all others and so individual that in criminal proceedings it may be accounted the surest distinguishing mark of the criminal.

"The development of personality from the germ-state to full consciousness is at once a charisma and a curse, because its first fruit is the conscious and unavoidable segregation of the single individual from the undifferentiated and unconscious herd. This means isolation, and there is no more comforting word for it. Neither family nor society nor position can save him from this fate, nor yet the most successful adaptation to his environment, however smoothly he fits in." [11] It is the isolation of the mature person, who no longer hangs upon the value judgments of his fellows but is firmly anchored in his relation to the Self. His knowledge that his dependence on something suprapersonal can never be wholly dissolved gives him security and support. It would nevertheless be a mistake to suppose that isolation in the sense of detachment from the mass also separates a man from his environment or from his neighbour. On the contrary, his relation to his fellow men becomes deeper, more tolerant, more responsible, and more understanding. He can open himself to them with greater freedom, since he need not fear that they will take possession of him, or that he will lose himself in them. In this sense Jung says: "Individuation does not shut one out from the world, but gathers the world to oneself." [12] "A real conflict with the collective norm arises only when an individual way is elevated to a norm, which is the actual aim of extreme individualism," [13] an attitude which Jung sharply repudiates.

So becoming what one essentially is does not mean turning

one's back on the collective, let alone adopting a hostile attitude towards it. It is only exaggerated adaptation and ingrati-
ation—as well as extreme rejection—that are to be avoided, as
they prevent any true contact. On the contrary, the man who is
capable of living his own way of life will fit in best and will
also be able to pay his tribute to society. He will not dissolve as
a particle in the mass but, as an individual, will become a responsible member of the community. And if fate makes him an
outsider, he will suffer it with humility and resignation, and
not injure others by rebelling against it.

For the realization of psychic wholeness it is indispensable
that the individual should free himself from the suggestive
power of the collective psyche as well as from that of the surrounding world and yet remain in conscious contact with
them. This means, on the one hand, that he must be able to
withstand the energy-laden contents of his collective unconscious, i.e., the archetypes, and, so far as they are constellated,
come to terms with them, while on the other hand recognizing
all the dubious, repressed, unlived, evil elements in his personal unconscious and accepting them as part of himself. He
must also learn to distinguish his ego from the collective consciousness, that is, from the spirit of the age and environmental
influences, and hold his own as an individual against the compulsion of convention and tradition, true to the law of his
being. One may even conclude with Jung: "Companionship
thrives only when each individual remembers his individuality
and does not identify with others." [14]

This holding one's own involves a series of unending but
quite conscious compromises and decisions, because the inner
and outer demands are often sharply opposed and throw the
ego into conflicts which can be overcome only by "growing
beyond" them. For this purpose, helpful powers are forthcoming from the unconscious. Just when one thinks that
the logic of a *tertium non datur* has barred the way to all
further progress, there emerge from the psychic background,
in dreams, fantasies, or intuitions, healing and whole-making

symbols of a successful union of opposites which overcome the supposed impasse. For it is a fact that unconscious tendencies, stirring unseen in the depths, betray their presence by all sorts of symbols long before they become conscious.[15] They appear, for instance, in waking fantasies and prove to be intuitions that point to a solution never before suspected. How often has one not found in a dream what the waking intellect could never discover, something apparently quite senseless which later turned out to be the saving factor! Thus the archetypal image of the "child", as a symbol of the pregnant beginning which, like a seed, already harbours within it the full flowering of the end, points to wholeness as the ultimate goal of man's development. In the same way the child, as a combination of the paternal and maternal substances and the unifier of their opposite natures, can often save a marriage from its apparently insurmountable antagonisms. In the life of the psyche, too, it is a reconciler of opposites and a symbol of unity and wholeness.

The often heard objection that individuation leads to individualism, egocentredness, eccentricity, etc., confuses individuation with a one-sided introversion. In individuation, inside and outside must both be given their due; it expresses, in Jung's words, a "successful adaptation to the universal conditions of existence coupled with the greatest possible freedom for self-determination".[16] It involves an attitude that can best be adopted by one who knows from personal experience to what degree the part is always obligated to the whole and yet remains a whole itself.

Again and again we can observe that as soon as an individual is threatened with the danger of isolation, there is a compensatory increase in the production of collective, archetypal symbols. They connect the isolated ego-consciousness, cut off from life, with the eternal images in the psychic background, with the layers that lie close to the instincts, where the whole experience of mankind is stored up and can give him succour. The two poles, ego and Self, which have grown too far apart, are thereby brought into living relationship again. Height and depth work on each other mutually, producing balance and security. Just as a high-standing tree, through its deep-reaching, wide-spreading roots, finds firm support in the earth that all trees share, so wherever healthy life prevails a regulating, balance-producing movement sets in. This is true also of the life of the psyche. And indeed the tree, with its upward and downward growth and its seasonal transformations, is often used as a symbol for the transformative processes of the psyche.[17]

Conscious Realization

Fᴿᴼᴹ the point of view of psychological development, the field of consciousness is extended through the analytical work by investigating and elucidating the material that comes up from the unconscious realm and associating it with consciousness. Extension of consciousness by supplementary material plus maturation by experience result in the development of the individual. In this process "conscious realization", also stipulated by other psychotherapeutic schools, is the ruling principle. The conscious realization of unconscious contents, their retention in consciousness, is the *sine qua non* of psychic development. "Conscious realization is culture in the broadest sense, and self-knowledge is therefore the heart and essence of this process," says Jung.[1] Nevertheless Jung's view differs from that of other schools in that it is grounded on the experience that the psyche, unless it is blocked by special circumstances, will spontaneously produce everything that is needed for the fulfilment of individual development.

We know that in dreams, for instance, powerful archetypal images will appear when consciousness has become too one-sided and run into a blind alley or "got stuck".[2] The ego then needs help in order to get out of its difficulties; it needs to be confronted with images and events which show it, in symbols, the typical human modes of behaviour appropriate to such ever-recurring situations. These images speak with the voice of nature that has always guided man. They have not been falsified by intellectual speculations or opinions, but are a source of age-old knowledge that is lacking in our impoverished present-day consciousness. This is true even of dreams that remain uninterpreted, for their dynamism and their symbols nevertheless have an effect on the psyche. Frequently they present their interpretation as it were of their own accord, bringing unexpected insights or intuitions that point the way ahead. But their numinosity can sometimes have a shattering effect, too. If, however, they are interpreted in the course of the analytical process they disclose their specific relationship to the actual psychic situation of the dreamer in all its aspects, which may have left deep furrows behind them. Their meaning can then be carefully worked out and substantiated.

If archetypal dreams and fantasies occur with great frequency, their powerful energy charge and wealth of symbols can threaten the psychic equilibrium and even overthrow it. They are a source of possible psychic transformation but also a threat to it. For this reason, particularly with young people, they are always danger signals and should be reduced to bearable proportions by concretizing their contents, that is, by writing them out or painting them, and whenever possible by understanding them. It is one of the main tasks of an analytically assisted individuation process to stimulate the symbol-producing capacity of the psyche and its natural tendency to self-regulation and assignment of meaning—in other words, to promote its "transcendent function".[3]

It is not an advantage, however, to have "big dreams" every night, for this is a sign that the psychic balance between the conscious and the unconscious realm is disturbed and that there is a danger of loss of relation to reality. If the ego is unable to assimilate the archetypal contents, which often irrupt into consciousness like foreign bodies, they can lead to delusions or even produce psychotic symptoms.[4] The ego is as it were "devoured" by the archetypal images, it identifies with them, can no longer distinguish itself from them. Then the individual fancies himself a religious or godlike figure, or a famous historical personality, or else something quite tiny—at all events a phenomenon deviating from normal human proportions. Much the same thing is true if we look at a group, a nation, or a race as one big individual. Technology and automation, the rejection of everything irrational, the over-abstract, theoretical trend of education in the West, and the resultant one-sided accentuation of consciousness, lead by way of compensation to an invasion of the ego by archetypal forces which can no longer be controlled by a consciousness cut off from its roots.

In the dialectical process between consciousness and the contents of the unconscious psyche, particular importance is attached to the dreams and associations of the analysand. They are considered under their personal and their suprapersonal aspects, i.e., given a meaningful interpretation and fitted into the context of his life. The more he perceives his unconscious qualities, qualities which either appear personified in the material of his dreams and fantasies or manifest themselves in projection on definite persons, the greater is his chance of gaining self-knowledge and accepting these projections as part of himself, withdrawing them and thus extending the scope of his field of consciousness. Above all the withdrawal of impersonal, archetypal projections and their conscious assimilation bring about an increase in knowledge and have a considerable effect on the ego personality, especially if the latter was hitherto unable to distinguish itself critically from the emergent contents that needed integrating, and allowed them no autonomy and no reality of their own.

There is an uninterrupted reciprocal action between the products of the unconscious psyche, manifesting themselves for instance in dreams and fantasies, symptomatic actions, "slips", and other such uncontrolled psychic phenomena, on the one hand, and consciousness, struggling to understand and integrate them, on the other. The analysis furthers and intensifies this reciprocal action by keeping the ego's contact with the deeper layers of the unconscious alive and fluid. But another dialectical process is going on at the same time between the psychic structure of the analysand and that of the analyst. In this process the human personality of both emerges more and more clearly, as a product of the creative background and at the same time as a conscious producer of this background.[5]

Transference and counter-transference,[6] i.e., the emotional tie of analysand to analyst and of analyst to analysand, and the proper way of dealing with them, are decisive factors in an analytically assisted individuation process. Jung says: "The main problem of medical psychotherapy is the *transference*. In this matter Freud and I were in complete agreement." [7] They were also in agreement as to the emotional relation of the analyst to the analysand being one of the most important ingredients of the analytical process. For not only must the patient, seeking help for his psychic troubles, make his full contribution to the common effort, but the analyst too must give his heart's blood if there is to be any development and transformation. Unless he does so, no real relationship of trust is established, and the result will remain correspondingly unsatisfactory.

It is very important—and this is no easy matter for the analyst—that he should be able to distinguish between the "objective truth" and the patient's "subjective truth", and accept the latter completely, as it alone has validity for the patient. This is the more difficult in that the two truths often contradict one another sharply. But the analyst, even though he knows this, should not show any mistrust nor should he contradict the patient, for in most cases it is a matter of projections which, with the help of the analyst's careful guidance, have to be realized and withdrawn. On his side, an active readiness to go along with the patient, a genuine psychic participation in what is happening, and objective goodwill towards him, are prerequisites for surmounting the obstacles that always arise in any individuation process, and for discussing and breaking down the extraordinarily strong resistances of the patient. This means that in every individuation assisted by analysis the analyst too will be drawn into the process of transformation, and this necessitates a continual regard not only for the personal but also, and more particularly, for the transpersonal, archetypal contents of the transference. It is indeed a heavy and responsible task, demanding constant alertness on the part of the analyst. Consequently, his degree of consciousness and psychic order are crucial factors in the individuation of the analysand.

Jung goes so far as to say that, if the process comes to a standstill and gets stuck, the analyst must seek the cause of the disturbance first of all in his own state of mind, in his own attitude. He used to quote a story about a Chinese rainmaker, who at a time of great drought was called to a village to make rain. For this purpose he withdrew to a lonely little hut for three days, asking only for some bread and water. On the fourth day a heavy rain fell. When they asked in astonishment how he did it, he replied: "I withdrew into myself and put myself in order; and when I am in order the world around me must naturally come into order too, and then the drought must be followed by rain." [8] This recipe does not always help, of course. Even when it is followed, it does not absolve the patient from devoting himself to the desired goal and making further efforts. Nevertheless one frequently finds that the dreams stop, for instance, because the last dream had been too little worked on, not interpreted properly. In such cases a renewed delving into the possible meaning of the dream may get the process moving again. Sometimes this even happens when the analyst does this work on his own. The attention he gives the patient's material, and his own efforts, may in themselves have a stimulating effect on the psychic processes going on in the patient.

No phase of the individuation process can be exchanged for another or skipped. If the demands of the first phase have been insufficiently considered in youth, they have to be caught up with later before the process can go ahead, and this means ad-

ditional pains of growing. Every conscious or unconscious attempt not to keep pace with the prescribed phases is doomed to
failure and means deviation, error, illness. Hence, too, the ripe
fruits of the way do not fall to youth but to age. The only
exceptions are those fates, those "short lives", where the individual stages often occur in compressed, abbreviated form. It
seems as though in these cases early death yet meant a relative
"rounding out" of psychic life.[9] The word "relative" needs
special emphasizing here. At bottom the individuation process,
as an event proceeding throughout life, is *never completed*. It
is a continual unending approach to a distant goal, death
being the ultimate boundary. Although, therefore, temporal
limits are set to wholeness by man's very existence, in its scope
it is unbounded, because the growth of components of the personality springs from an unconscious realm to which no
boundaries can be assigned.

This unconscious realm of the psyche can in practice never
be "emptied". Only a comparatively small part of it can be
made conscious, and this part too varies in size according to the
individual's capacity and readiness for experience. The notion
that everything in the unconscious can in principle be made
conscious is a logical consequence of the assumption that everything unconscious was once conscious and has been repressed.[10]
With Jung's conception of the collective unconscious and its
archetypes, which do not contain repressed material but are
genuine propensities to certain modes of action and reaction
ingrained in the species, the idea of complete conscious realization could refer at most—and then only to a limited degree—
to the contents of the personal unconscious. Into this realm of
the psyche falls everything we have forgotten, or have sublim-
inally perceived, everything we have suppressed or repressed,
so that the unconscious background of the psyche is constantly
being filled up again. Nevertheless by far the greatest part of
the psyche, above all the collective unconscious, will continue
to remain unconscious. Everything that is unlived, unsolved,
unexperienced, obscure, and mysterious will remain behind
and form the matrix for germs of new possibilities.

Moreover a very far-reaching consciousness can become a
burden, and for this reason too it is feared and avoided. As the
capacity for judgment grows in proportion to the scope of consciousness, it burdens a man with a growing sense of responsibility. It is therefore understandable that the growth of consciousness is resisted almost automatically, by the very inertia
of nature. An illustration of this is the Oriental fairytale of the
blind king who promised his kingdom and his treasure to the
man who could make him see. And in fact a wonder-working
doctor came along and gave him his sight back. But a year
later the king was already in deep despair. As he now possessed
nothing but his beautiful daughter, his only child, he promised her to the man who could help to make him blind again.
But no such person could be found. The king had to remain
sighted, as once Adam and Eve, having eaten of the tree of
knowledge, could not recapture their unconsciousness, and humanity ever afterwards had to go forward willy-nilly on the
road of conscious realization, which is often a very painful one.

Observation and assimilation, conscious realization and acceptance—that is what is demanded. "Every step forward in culture is, psychologically speaking, an extension of consciousness,
a conscious realization which cannot come about except by discrimination. Any progress therefore always begins with individuation, that is, with a single individual, conscious of his
isolation, breaking a new way through regions hitherto un-
trodden. For this he must first reflect on the basic facts of his
life—regardless of all authority and tradition—and become
conscious of his distinctiveness." [11] This is an extremely hard
demand, especially for Western man, who early has inculcated
into him the hybris of the will and is accustomed to judge everything by prefabricated standards consisting mostly of prejudices, preconceived opinions, and collective regulations. Everything is labelled "good", "bad", "right", "wrong", etc., before
one has a chance to reflect on its true nature, its purpose and
value, and form a judgment of one's own.

It is characteristic of the maladjusted person, the neurotic in
particular, that he cannot accept himself as he is by nature,

and chastises himself with whips and scorpions in order to make himself what he is not and cannot be, the result of this fruitless attempt at adaptation being that he is finally neither the one thing nor the other. Hence it is one of the most important requirements in analytical work that the analyst should, to begin with, accept the person who entrusts himself to him just as he is, should accept his nature as the one that belongs to him, should not play the teacher or judge but should be an understanding companion. His job is to hold up a mirror to the patient in which he can see his rejected qualities, but can also learn that he must accept them as belonging to himself for his individuation. This naturally does not mean that he can live them and act them out freely, as the opponents of depth psychology think; but it does mean remaining conscious of these qualities instead of repressing them again with a view to convincing himself that he does not possess them. It is not by repression or by forcible suppression that they can be brought under control, but by insight and self-reflection.

Nothing can be gained in individuation by force of will or by preconceived opinions; our task consists simply and solely in keeping the conscious mind constantly on the alert, so that as many of the unconscious portions of the personality as possible can be made conscious, experienced, and integrated. "The needful thing is not to 'know' the truth but to *experience* it. Not to have an intellectual conception of things, but to find our way to the inner, perhaps wordless, irrational experiences —that is the heart of the problem," says Jung.[12]

For individuation is a spontaneous process of development independent of conscious volition, a process in which the ego has not only to experience and understand the contents of the non-ego[13] but also to suffer them with open eyes. Pain and suffering are an organic part of it. They are inexorable necessities, symbolically represented by the *mortificatio* in alchemy, the "night sea journey" in the belly of the whale-monster,[14] the self-incineration of the phoenix, or the journey through the underworld in Dante's *Divine Comedy*.

In the individuation process it is always a matter of something obsolete that must be left behind to die in order that the new may be born. Not only in alchemy, but in myths and fairytales as well, we see how the "old king", the representative of the traditional, conventional attitude of consciousness, must either die or abdicate because a renewal has become necessary. Then the son or the young hero takes his place; he ascends the throne, because he stands for a level of conscious development more appropriate to the times. This "take-over" is usually not without its difficulties. Usually it begins with a "descent into the underworld", involving numerous trials and feats such as are described so impressively in the hero-myths. The throne must be won, victory hard fought for; every step forward demands its sacrifice.

As between consciousness and the unconscious, so a dialectical relationship also exists between turning inwards and conscious participation in the inner happenings, and turning outwards and consolidation of what has been won in the outside world. The attitude-type of the individual is irrelevant in this connection. "Western man seems predominantly extraverted, Eastern man predominantly introverted. The former projects the meaning and considers that it exists in objects; the latter feels the meaning in himself. But the meaning is both without and within." [15] To surrender oneself to both realms is essential to the full experience of the individuation process. Jung expressly emphasizes: "The new thing never came exclusively either from within or from without. If it came from outside, it became a profound inner experience; if it came from inside, it became an outer happening. In no case was it conjured into existence intentionally or by conscious willing, but seemed rather to be borne along on the stream of time." [16]

All this demands patience and preparedness. Not, to be sure, "passive" patience, but a forbearance from the presumption of the will that dominates so many people—a modesty and willingness, rather, to let things happen and ripen instead of arguing and passing value judgments. Another important quality is courage—courage to live, to experience, to dare. It is one thing to read a passionate romance, quite another to fall head over heels in love; one thing to study a scientific paper on pneumonia, quite another to have it and endure it. Unfortunately it is characteristic of the neurotic to "think" life in all its details, but not to experience it in his own body. He shuns all the imponderables of existence whenever he can and seeks security against dangers, even surprises being felt as "dangerous". Thus, for want of the psychic strength won in the battle of life, he is usually oppressed and beset by fear, and not infrequently hopes to raise himself to a higher level of existence by "meditation". He does not notice, or refuses to notice, that in so doing he has only withdrawn into a fear-ridden passivity. Nor does he notice how much he avoids anything unaccustomed, for which reason he is even afraid of the as yet untried state of being cured of his neurosis. "Whoever protects himself against what is new and strange and regresses to the past falls into the same neurotic condition as the man who identifies himself with the new and runs away from the past. The only difference is that the one has estranged himself from the past and the other from the future. In principle both are doing the same thing: they are reinforcing their narrow range of consciousness instead of shattering it in the tension of opposites and building up a state of wider and higher consciousness." [17]

The analytically assisted individuation process demands from every individual full participation in outer life as well as in inner life. No risk and no suffering should be shunned; one must face everything that comes and hold out against fate. Hence analytical work is not, as many people expect, an undivided joy, a walk in sunny fields; it is more often a painful process, wearisome and finicking, in which the life and insights we have missed must be made up for item by item, and this ability to live open-eyed with one's own darkness is an achievement that demands courage above everything.

Here we come upon an apparent contradiction, but one that disappears on closer inspection. On the one hand, it is said, if one undergoes an individuation process one must "let things happen", submit, humbly give in; on the other hand one must not sidestep any risk, must spare oneself no effort. As a matter of fact both attitudes are required, both belong to the individuation process, depending on the situation of the psyche and on external circumstances. If the ego is caught in a seemingly hopelessly conflict, or has landed itself in a cul-de-sac, guidance must be handed over to the inner authority, the Self; if the ego is still capable, after careful reflection, of finding a way out of the impasse, however thorny, then the second form of behaviour is indicated.

We are confronted with two possible situations. In the second situation the ego has to take the lead and decide, having regard, however, to the advice, statements, and needs of the unconscious psychic background. Acting in this way, a man escapes from the compulsion of his autonomous impulses, from the danger of being driven and overpowered by them. But if he is in the first situation, the ego, being unable to decide, to judge, to act, must entrust itself or submit to the guidance of the unknown, or the unconscious—in religious terms, to the guidance of God, even if things happen that bring more suffering. This means a relative depotentiation of the sovereignty of the ego, which is permissible *only* as a final decision in insoluble conflicts between two possible courses of action. The individuation process thus has a double sign: active endeavour and a consciously endured "come what may" are connected in a dialectical relationship.

"Letting things happen", listening to the inner voice, is something that the neurotic above all has to learn, as an unadapted person who wants to compel fate with his will. He seems to be still under the spell of magical ideas, ascribing to his thoughts almighty powers as a consequence of which he is plagued by corresponding feelings of anxiety. On the other hand, one must be careful and not, as a reaction against overvaluing the will, go to the other extreme of letting oneself be influenced and guided solely by the promptings of the un-

conscious. How urgent and essential the extension of the field
of consciousness is, is proved by the fact that the freedom of
the will is proportionate to the degree of a man's consciousness.
This is a fact of ethical importance. The freedom of the will
extends only as far as the limits of consciousness; as soon as
these limits are overstepped, we cease to discriminate, to be
capable of conscious choice and judgment, and are delivered
over to the uncontrolled impulses and tendencies of the unconscious.

It is therefore the foremost task of consciousness—and this is
a possibility specific only to man—to assimilate what comes out
of the unconscious depths. "If this does not happen," says
Jung, "the process of individuation will nevertheless continue.
The only difference is that we become its victims and are
dragged along by fate towards that inescapable goal which we
might have reached by walking upright, if only we had taken
the trouble and been patient enough to understand in time
the meaning of the numina that cross our path." [18] Instead of
meeting the demands of individuation consciously and of our
own free will, instead of going the "royal way" of life, we go
the way of the herd, blind and will-less, and remain retarded
in our psychic development.

The number of individuals who are capable at all of attain-
ing psychic wholeness is, of course, veiled from our knowledge.
Equally, "we do not know what the suggestive power of an
extended consciousness may be, or what influence it may have
upon the world at large".[19] In Jung's view the "change of
consciousness begins at home; it is an age-long process that
depends entirely on how far the psyche's capacity for development extends".[20] Perhaps there is—one might add—an increase of consciousness in humanity as a whole, but at the cost
of the "natural psyche" of the individual. Those who experience the individuation process with open eyes will surely be
able to strike the golden mean. For "the true art of living is the
middle way between yieldingness and rigidity".[21]

It should not be forgotten that, despite the causal nexus in which he lives, man also possesses a feeling of freedom that is identical with the autonomy of consciousness. This is the Danaän gift of his disobedience in Paradise, of his eating of the tree of knowledge. Jung says: "However much the ego can be proved to be dependent and preconditioned, it cannot be convinced that it has no freedom . . . The existence of ego-consciousness has meaning only if it is free and autonomous. By stating these facts we have, it is true, established an antinomy, but we have at the same time given a picture of things as they are. There are temporal, local and individual differences in the degree of dependence and freedom. In reality both are always present: the supremacy of the self and the hybris of consciousness. This conflict between conscious and unconscious is at least brought nearer to a solution through our becoming aware of it." [22] Without consciousness we would not even know whether this world existed or not; and without the unconscious portion of the psyche the source of all good and evil, of all that is old and all that is new, of all beauty and ugliness, would be lost.

Conscious realization really begins with the dawn of man's history. At first there was an undivided harmony of plant, animal, man, and God, which pervaded everything and has been handed down to us in the symbol of Paradise. Man lived then in the blissful state of unconsciousness, of spacelessness and timelessness, as though in the lap of God, at one with him, in him. With the eating of the forbidden fruit, by which he "knew" good and evil, i.e., became conscious, man's earthly life as we understand it began. From then on, expelled from Paradise, torn between his conscious, individual ego and the unconscious depths of his soul still reposing in God, he had to make his way back with toil and suffering to the original unity, in order to reach it, perhaps, at the end of time—but this time in the full light of his consciousness. Not for nothing does the Bible story of the creation represent that first coming of human consciousness as the infringement of a taboo, as though

with the winning of knowledge a sacrosanct, inviolable bound
had been overstepped.

For that step towards concious realization was a sort of Pro-
methean guilt: "Through knowledge, the gods are as it were
robbed of their fire, that is, something that was the property of
the unconscious powers is torn out of its natural context and
subordinated to the whims of the conscious mind. The man
who has usurped the new knowledge suffers, however, a transformation or enlargement of consciousness, which no longer
resembles that of his fellow men. He has raised himself above
the human level of his age ('ye shall become like unto God,
knowing good and evil'), but in doing so has alienated himself
from humanity." [23] He has become an individual with his own
fate, lonely and threatened with punishment. It was sin, arro-
gance, to know himself apart from God, to confront him face
to face, and thus break the law of the unity of all things in
primal night. "And yet the attainment of consciousness was the
most precious fruit of the tree of knowledge, the magical
weapon which gave man victory over the earth, and which we
hope will give him a still greater victory over himself." [24]

For "life that just happens in and for itself is not real life: it
is real only when it is *known*. Only a unified personality can
experience life, not that personality which is split up into partial aspects, that bundle of odds and ends which also calls itself
'man'." [25] That is why the "natural" as well as the "analytically
assisted" individuation process seeks to reunite what was divided, the light and the dark side of the psyche, to restore to
man his wholeness by a continual widening of consciousness,
and not to deepen the split between them by accentuating
their one-sidedness but to bring about their union by bridging
the opposites.

There are still many people today who are only partially conscious. A relatively large number are almost completely unconscious and spend their lives mostly in an unconscious condition.
They suffer what happens to them, but are not conscious
of what they do and say, they do not know the significance

of their deeds and words and can give no account of it. The extension of consciousness is still hedged about by fear, still surrounded by the breath of original sin, and is therefore dreaded and avoided. And yet: "The world comes into being when man discovers it. He discovers it when he sacrifices the 'mother', that is, when he comes out of the mists of his unconscious containment in the mother." [26] "The coming of consciousness was probably the most tremendous experience of primeval times, for with it a world came into being whose existence no one had suspected before. 'And God said: Let there be light!' is the projection of that immemorial experience of the separation of the conscious from the unconscious." [27]

Jung himself calls it a "confession of faith" when he says: "I believe that, after thousands and millions of years, someone had to realize that this wonderful world of mountains and oceans, suns and moons, galaxies and nebulae, plants and animals, *exists*. From a low hill in the Athi plains of East Africa I once watched the vast herds of wild animals grazing in the soundless stillness, as they had done from time immemorial . . . The entire world around me was still in its primeval state; it did not know that it *was*. And then, in that one moment in which I came to know, the world sprang into being . . . All Nature seeks this goal and finds it fulfilled in man, but only in the most highly developed and most fully conscious man." [28] Thus the wantonness which Adam and Eve committed became the source of all spiritual growth and drives us forward on the way to an ever higher development of the psyche and our world, to a consciousness of our relation to God and his workings in the soul through the symbols of the Self.

The Religious Function
and Conscience

THE outcome of an individuation process to which a man has devoted himself with all his powers is an attitude that one can rightly call "religious" in the proper sense of the word. For this process leads him to the knowledge that he is at the mercy of an irrational power which transcends his consciousness and which he has to accept humbly. To this power he has given a great variety of names. By Christians it is called "God", in whose image man was created.[1] He imagines this God as a person of transcendent and metaphysical nature. Conscious of his dependence upon him, he knows also his own earthly measure and can understand himself in right proportion to God and his creation.

The ability to believe is a function given to man at birth.[2] His special directedness to God is, in Jung's view, an autochthonous religious urge, an inborn need of the soul, which cannot be neglected or violated without grave injury to psychic health. For him every neurosis is basically an expression of a disturbance of the "religious function" of the psyche, which he regards as its fundamental function. If it is inhibited or blocked, man fashions substitute gods for himself, and, succumbing to them, impoverishes his inner life, with congruent psychic disturbances.[3] This works out disastrously, particularly in the second half of life. For whereas a young person has to devote his whole attention to adapting to the demands of outer reality, after middle life a man is turned more and more strongly to his inner depths, to his relation to God, whom he must face at death. That is why in this phase of life the question of a religious anchorage becomes an urgent problem which can no longer be avoided.

The individuation process is directed first and foremost to the completeness of the personality. Its constant aim is to raise out of unconsciousness the "missing" element that would make for wholeness, and to join it to consciousness. In our materialistically oriented world, therefore, the prime task will be spiritualization, the *opus contra naturam*. If, however, a man lives too one-sidedly, in the intellect alone, which is nothing but pseudo-spirit, then the work of individuation will address itself partly to the "right" spirit and partly to the inclusion of "Nature" and a recognition of the values of the world of instinct. Since both kinds of work demand the sacrifice of one-sidedness, whether of spirit or of Nature, both need that attitude of humility which we may call "religious". This consists on the one hand in the knowledge of our dependence on fate, and on the other hand in the knowledge that every step that takes us nearer to wholeness can be made only *Deo concedente*.

Ultimately, all religious belief is a charisma. It falls to us as a gift of grace and can never be forced by the will. It comes upon one unawares, and often possesses one completely. "Religious experience is absolute," says Jung, "it cannot be disputed. You can only say that you have never had such an experience, whereupon your opponent will reply: 'Sorry, I have.' And there your discussion will come to an end." [4] And elsewhere: "Theology does not help those who are looking for the key, because theology demands faith, and faith cannot be made: it is in the truest sense a gift of grace. We moderns are faced with the necessity of rediscovering the life of the spirit; we must experience it anew for ourselves." [5] For Jung, then, the experience of God in the form of an encounter or *unio mystica* is the only possible and authentic way to a genuine belief in God for modern man.

The individuation process can "prepare" a man for such an

experience. It can open him to the influence of a world beyond his rational consciousness, and give him insight into it. Any thorough analytical work on the psychic material will have to push forward to the individual's religious attitude, and will awaken, clarify, or deepen this attitude, as the case may be. A false or inadequate religious attitude will be unmasked, and even a relatively genuine faith can be thrown into a crisis of decision.[6] This is particularly important in the case of a faith that is too rigid, narrow, and dogmatic, if the individual is to gain an inwardly freer attitude and have a personal experience of his relationship to God.[7]

In place of speculative knowledge, which is alien to faith, the individuation process can convey an empirical knowledge which is not mere religiosity, thoughtlessly imitated and as it were grafted on to a person, but a living relation to God, validated by the experience itself. "So long as religion is only faith and outward form, and the religious function is not experienced in our own souls, nothing of any importance has happened. It has yet to be understood that the *mysterium magnum* is not only an actuality but is first and foremost rooted in the human psyche," says Jung.[8] He thinks that access to faith is blocked for the man of today because the eternal images in which the mystery of faith is expressed are largely lost. Modern man's understanding for the "precious vessels of the mystery of faith",[9] the symbols, is obscured. Thus in analytical work "the field of the soul must be ploughed up, that the word of God may take root".[10] "It is man's opportunity that God does not leave him in peace and has implanted in his psyche the prime function of faith, which ever seeks a place where it may feel at home." [11]

In the religious function of the psyche, the activity of the Self is revealed in its most significant aspect, often assuming a fateful character. The religious function is, therefore, closely bound up with the role which the manifestation of the Self plays in every individual life. Like the Self, it may remain unrecognized for long periods, or assume strange "disguised" forms. It is not simply a product of the analytically assisted individuation process; rather, it is the motor that drives a man to the completion of his human task, and the individuation process to its fulfilment.

It is a matter of indifference for psychic health what religion or creed a person professes, whether he wishes to remain outside them all and to create his own particular relation to God. From the psychological point of view, a man can become psychically balanced and advance towards psychic wholeness whether as a Mohammedan or a Buddhist, a Jew or a Christian. The one decisive thing is that each should win to a form of faith corresponding to his own nature, based on an entirely personal judgment and sense of responsibility, which sustains him from then on and gives him inner security. One might say that in the course of the individuation process a man arrives at the entrance to the house of God. Whether he opens the door and penetrates to the inner sanctuary where the divine images are, this last step is left to him alone. He may, after having encountered on his journey the reality of the religious numina and experienced their shattering effect in his personal life or in dreams, turn aside from them in resistance and deny them, or else make them his innermost possession.

The individuation process can prepare the way for such insights and decisions. It is, however, not its task to bring about a conversion or to advocate a particular creed. In Jung's view that does not lie within the competence of the analyst, and must be left to the priest or theologian. For individuation is a psychological goal and not a religious one, although it can be reached only by including a religious attitude.

Jung has never been concerned with faith in a confessional sense, much less with "having to believe", but rather with an openness to the irrational beyond our human grasp. On the other hand, he has sought to make man habitually conscious of the limits of the ego in order to secure him a place in this world suited to his finiteness. Consciousness is not denied its leading role: on the contrary, it remains the decisive authority, even when its decision must be to leave leadership to the impersonal powers that determine man's fate. Here Jung is not dabbling in metaphysics, nor does he discuss the contents of faith as such. Conscious of his limitations, he says: "Psychology is concerned with the act of seeing and not with the construction of new religious truths, when even the existing teachings have not yet been perceived and understood. In religious matters it is a well-known fact that we cannot understand a thing until we have experienced it inwardly." [12]

Jung is interested simply and solely in understanding religious statements as empirical psychological phenomena. What religious experience or metaphysical truth may be *in itself* he does not pretend to know in his capacity as psychologist and psychotherapist. "Looked at empirically, they are essentially psychic phenomena, that is, they manifest themselves as such and must therefore be submitted to psychological criticism, evaluation, and investigation." [13] Only then can they be grasped by the conscious mind and given a worthy place in the structure of the psyche. For "the more unconscious we are of the religious problem in the future, the greater the danger of our putting the divine germ within us to some ridiculous or demoniacal use, puffing ourselves up with it instead of remaining conscious that we are no more than the manger in which the Lord is born".[14]

The religious function of the psyche is closely connected with the problem of conscience. If it is disturbed, if it is not perceived or is suppressed, the psychic economy is thrown into disorder and man makes himself the measure of all things. He becomes presumptuous, and is seized by a hybris of the will. He falls a victim to inflation, or to a depression just as deep. Vainly he tries to live up to the precepts and laws that hold sway in the outer world. Nowhere does he feel safe and secure, his conscience gives him no rest. Again and again it calls him to self-reflection.

Jung has, in general, regarded neurotic and psychotic dis-

turbances as symptoms of deviation from the natural maturation demanded by the psyche, which is, as it were, its religious
destiny. It seemed to him that the meaning of these psychic
sufferings might consist in their compelling a man to come to
terms with the foundations of his being and with the world,
and thereby to gain a better knowledge of his limits and possibilities as well as broadening his consciousness. Jung thus put
the emphasis on the prospective aspect, giving neurosis a positive meaning and not regarding it only as a burdensome illness. According to him, it can even act as a stimulus in the
struggle for the development of the personality and be, paradoxically, a curative factor. Not only the sufferer, but every
questing and striving person, will involuntarily feel the neglect
or violation of the task imposed on him by nature—the maturation of the personality—as "guilt". Although the fear of not
living up to the demands and expectations of the collective
may cause him pangs of conscience, he is beset by the deepest
feelings of guilt if he fails to mature according to his age.

Conscience for Jung, in contrast to Freud,[15] is thus only to
a limited extent an authority conditioned by social commands
and prohibitions; it is rather a structural quality inborn in the
psyche, directed to the maintenance of the psychic balance and
aiming at its wholeness. It rises up warningly against any ob-
stacle put in the way of this goal, both in the "natural" individuation process and in the "analytically assisted" one. Its
voice can be heard imperatively when it brings a man into
conflict with the conventional moral law and confronts him
with the choice between his own individual way and the collective way of tradition.

In these cases Jung speaks of a genuine "conflict of duty",
when one's duty to the social or even professional norm is in-
compatible with one's duty to one's own personality. We know
from experience that man's innate impulses are not always in
accord with the so-called moral code. Often they are completely at variance with it, if one regards the moral code as the
traditional religious and moral views of a given environment

at a given time. In the terminology of Freud it would, to a certain extent, correspond to the "superego", and in Jung's to the "collective consciousness". But over and above that, Jung also takes account of the influence of the inherited, instinctive modes of behaviour, the archetypes, which, uninfluenced by the will or by consciousness, represent the necessities of human nature and in many people's conscience manifest themselves as the *vox Dei,* the voice of God. In this case, man conducts himself not according to the accepted moral code, but according to guiding lines laid down in the unconscious foundations of his personality: "The decision is drawn from dark and deep waters." [16] Thus often, though not always, the insight of the conscious ego, which wants to obey the accepted moral principles, and the inner voice, which wants to maintain or restore the psychic equilibrium, are directly opposed and each wants to conquer the other. The ego, meanwhile, finds itself in the situation of Buridan's ass, who had to choose between two bundles of hay. It is only this conflict situation, i.e., the above-mentioned "conflict of duty", that calls up genuine problems of conscience, according to Jung.

In order to distinguish between these two forms of conscience, the collective and the individual, Jung proposes that the first be called the "moral" aspect of conscience and the second the "ethical" aspect. "Conscience is a psychic reaction which one can call *moral* because it always appears when the conscious mind leaves the path of custom, or the *mores,* or suddenly recollects it." [17] "Distinct from this is the ethical form of conscience, which appears when two decisions or ways of acting, both affirmed to be moral and therefore regarded as 'duties', collide with one another. In these cases, not foreseen by the moral code because they are mostly very individual, a judgment is required which cannot properly be called 'moral' or in accord with custom." [18] Most people know conscience only in its first form; only a few experience genuine conflicts of duty which set them against collective morality. To avoid the responsibilities of a personal decision, which would mean giving the "ethical" conscience priority over the "moral" conscience, most people repress the conflict and all too often end up with a neurosis.

A special problem is presented by the fact that one cannot make out in advance whether the voice of conscience is "right" or "wrong". For evil, disguised in the admonitions of conscience, can prompt us from within to deeds and reactions unworthy of man. One has only to think, for instance, of Hitler's conviction that the command for the liquidation of the Jews sprang from his conscience.

It is a common experience that deviation from the moral code is attended by great dangers. For this reason all religions have established rules of conduct whose non-observance may drive man into the severest conflicts. The conflict situations into which we are thrown by our inner impulses and the reactions of conscience put us in a paradoxical, divisive psychic state, but for which the question of conscience would present no problem at all, since in moral matters one could then rely entirely on the decision of the inner voice.[19] "The primitive form of conscience is paradoxical," says Jung. "Both forms of conscience, the right and the false, stem from the same source, and both therefore have approximately the same power of conviction." [20] This "source" is the archetype of the God-image, the Self, which dwells in the depths of the soul and is by nature polaristic, containing light and shadow in equal degree.[21]

The point here is Jung's view that conscience, like the religious function, possesses a quality that aids conscious realization and aims at individual self-development, i.e., at individuation. Any deviation from the way of individuation, from the demands laid upon man by his "destiny", can provoke a reaction of conscience. Conscience, therefore, has an important task in the development of the individual, keeping watch over it and urging it towards its goal. But, if he is to be a complete human being, he must do justice equally to the collective "moral" demands and the individual "ethical" demands, and thus be essentially a paradox. However, it is just this paradoxicality that accords most fully with his nature. For "there is scarcely any other psychic phenomenon that shows the polarity of the psyche in a clearer light than conscience," says Jung.[22] According to him, the polaristic structure of the psyche is the foundation of psychic life and keeps it in a state of constant dynamic tension.

Whereas obedience to the "moral" conscience can at least be sure of the approval of society, following the dictates of the "ethical" conscience remains the responsibility of the individual and exposes him to the danger of going astray. Unfortunately, "In practice it is very difficult to indicate the exact point at which the 'right' conscience stops and the 'false' one begins, and what the criterion is that divides the one from the other." [23]

Conscience may indeed demand that the individual follow his inner voice even at the risk of going astray. If he refuses to obey it, and, for fear of taking the wrong road, adapts to the generally accepted, traditional morality, he will nevertheless feel uneasy because he has been untrue to his real nature. His adaptation will be forced and his "ethical" conscience will continue to plague him until "a creative solution emerges which . . . is in accord with the deepest foundations of the personality as well as with its wholeness; it embraces conscious and unconscious and therefore transcends the ego" by producing a "third standpoint" that bridges the opposites.[24] It goes without saying that confusion and error cannot be avoided. Yet this must be accepted by anyone who has submitted himself to the pains of the individuation process. For it is not only a "road of endless compromises", the "middle road", but also a quest, a thorny path strewn with mistakes and wrong deeds that also have to be experienced. They too have their function; they help us to insights that broaden and deepen the field of consciousness, and we know that they are the precondition of any further development.

Thus conscience becomes a monitor urging us to a confrontation with the world within and without, the examiner of the genuineness of our deeds and behaviour, the messenger between the "voice of God" and our consciousness. People who declare they have no conscience because they never hear its call are as good as dead, for their psychic life is extinct.

Experience shows that the achievement demanded by the analytically assisted individuation process—the resolute courage to face and endure one's own darkness—is forthcoming only in exceptional cases. The price that has to be paid seems too high for most people. For this reason they remain stuck in a more or less unconscious state and live without reflecting in the mist of *participation mystique* with the surrounding world. "What is it, in the end, that induces a man to go his own way and to rise out of unconscious identity with the mass as out of a swathing mist? . . . It is what is commonly called *vocation*: an irrational factor that destines a man to emancipate himself from the herd and from its well-worn paths . . . Vocation acts like a law of God from which there is no escape . . . Anyone with a vocation hears the voice of the inner man: he is *called*." [25] "What would have happened if Paul had allowed himself to be talked out of his journey to Damascus?" Jung asks.[26] "Unless one accepts one's fate . . . there is no individuation; one remains a mere accident, a mortal nothing." [27] That is why those people who have been most deeply affected by the problems and images of the psychic background cannot but feel, looking back on their lives, that their path of development could not have been otherwise.

Not following one's destiny, or trying to avoid one's fate, is a frequent cause of numerous psychic difficulties. It may even be that the steady increase in the number of neurotics today is due to the fact that more and more individuals are called upon by fate to work for their psychic wholeness, but that fewer and fewer of them are ready to do so. Any obstruction of the natural process of development, any avoidance of the law of life, or getting stuck on a level unsuited to one's age, takes its revenge, if not immediately, then later at the onset of the second half of

life, in the form of serious crises, nervous breakdowns, and all
manner of physical and psychic sufferings. Mostly they are accompanied by vague feelings of guilt, by tormenting pangs of
conscience, often not understood, in face of which the individual is helpless. He knows he is not guilty of any bad deed, he
has not given way to any illicit impulse, and yet he is plagued
by uncertainty, discontent, despair, and above all by anxiety—
a constant, indefinable anxiety. And in truth he must usually
be pronounced "guilty". His guilt does not lie in the fact that
he has a neurosis, but in the fact that, knowing he has one, he
does nothing to set about curing it.

This also explains why many practising Catholics do not feel
freed by confession and absolution, but go on being oppressed
and persecuted by fears. And indeed they cannot confess anything except what lies consciously on their conscience, while
they are not conscious of their real guilt at all; it is not anything they have done or thought, essentially it is ungraspable
and can hardly be put into words. For it relates to their whole
previous life, to which they did not pay its due tribute; it relates to the "destiny" that was laid upon them but was not
lived, to the psychic development they missed, which their nature would yet have made possible. The fact that they remained infantile, their one-sidedness and the neglect of their
other qualities, their fear of taking the plunge into life, their
constant prevarication and criticism—all this and a lot more
besides are the cause of guilt feelings and pangs of conscience
which never let them go.

To submit to an individuation process as a conscious decision is therefore, in Jung's view, not only a way of developing
one's own nature, but a psychotherapeutic necessity for all
those who suffer from afflictions of the soul.

The Dual Nature of Man

Although the word "individuation" is much in the air nowadays, it is surprising how few people have a correct picture of it. Most of them still think that "individuating" means becoming a sort of superman, who has absolute power over his instincts, who is entirely spiritualized, who loves everybody and whom everybody loves, selfless, always ready to help, always just and good, etc., etc.—in a word, a man who has attained perfection. It is not difficult to recognize in this picture the traditional Christian ideal imprinted on the West and held up to us all in childhood as the goal of our character. Those who are moulded by this ideal have no doubt whatever about the rightness of their views and convictions and are full of resistances when one tries to make clear to them that the consequences of an individuation process, as understood by Jung, may quite as well consist in one's becoming, in comparison with the aforementioned ideal picture, less "good" and "perfect" than one was before, but, instead, more "complete" and "whole".

The individuation process has in no sense a "moral" goal in the accepted meaning of the word. It does not aim at perfectionism, but only at helping a man to become in the truest sense what he in fact is, and not to hide behind the ideal mask which is so easily mistaken for his true essence, although by so doing he makes it all the more likely that the evil repressed behind it will break out. We should perhaps rather remember that the individuation process has in Jung's view an "ethical" goal, reminding ourselves that, in this context, Jung uses the word "morality" to denote what accords with the *mores,* with the social order, whereas by "ethics" he means that essential and fundamental nature to which man is oriented by the universal order.[1] Man in this world is committed to, and has to submit to, both orders, but since they often get into insoluble conflicts with one another he must learn to endure these conflicts as well.

The endeavour to follow the rules and regulations in every way, whether pedagogical, social, or ecclesiastical, and nowhere to stumble, much less commit a "sin", is a perfectionism that all too often leads not to perfection but to a neurosis instead. For it does violence to the natural make-up of man, which, though it strives for the good and the right, also has in it potentialities for the evil and the wrong. Human imperfection, which clings to every one of us since the expulsion from Paradise, from that unconscious containment in and oneness with God, can presumably be sloughed off only through an act of divine grace. Grace, however, can fall to the lot also of the man who in our estimation is unworthy, for the ways of God and his reasons are not to be discovered by our earthly probings, nor can they be grasped or interpreted psychologically.

Even in the Lord's Prayer we petition God not to lead us into temptation, thus confessing that our sinfulness may perhaps be permitted or actually willed by God in order to test us, to confront us with our "fallen" nature so that we may become fully conscious of it. In the first chapter of the Book of Job, Satan is counted among the "sons of God".[2] He has the task of making a trial of man, of humbling him in order to show him his sinfulness. He thus has a dark but necessary role to play in God's plan of salvation.[3] And because Satan goes to and fro upon the earth and is always in our midst, every man has in the background of his soul—for only a few can tolerate a clear consciousness of their sinful nature—an obscure feeling of guilt and sin. That is why the Catholic Church wisely instituted the practice of confession and absolution, for in this way even the most unconscious man can be made to realize his fallibility, thus giving him an impetus towards transformation and rebirth.

At any rate, says Jung, "to strive after τελείωσις—completion—in this sense is not only legitimate but is inborn in man as a peculiarity which provides civilization with one of its strongest roots." [4] Only if a man thinks he can actually be perfect, that is, become like God, will life again and again bring about his downfall. He must constantly run up against his limits lest he become too arrogant. Jung mournfully admits: "The individual may strive after perfection . . . but must suffer from the opposite of his intentions for the sake of his completeness." [5] This suffering can be a powerful spur to his further striving and hold him to the road of his inner development. One must agree with Jung when he says: "There is no light without shadow and no psychic wholeness without imperfection. To round itself out, life calls not for perfection but for completeness; and for this the 'thorn in the flesh' is needed, the suffering of defects without which there is no progress and no ascent." [6] "When one follows the path of individuation, when one lives one's own life, one must take mistakes into the bargain; life would not be complete without them. There is no guarantee—not for a single moment—that we will not fall into error or stumble into deadly peril. We may think there is a safe road. But that would be the road of death. Then nothing happens any longer—at any rate, not the right things. Anyone who takes the safe road is as good as dead." [7]

This conviction of Jung's has provoked much resistance and given rise to countless misunderstandings, since in the West the striving for perfection belongs to the inventory of a religious upbringing and education. Many people easily fall into the error of believing that perfection is attainable in principle here on earth, and forget that it is at most something to be aimed at. Though it can be approached, it can never be reached. The dark counterpole, however strongly it be suppressed or repressed, is only shamming dead; it lives on in the depths of the psyche and invisibly influences everything we humans are and do, feel and believe. Without this dark hinterland man remains two-dimensional, and the more he tries to rid himself of it the less complete he becomes. Filled out by his "other side", admitting its existence and recognizing its influence, he becomes complete. He is what he knows of himself, his conscious ego-side, but besides that he is what he *also* is, the potential he has not realized, and what lies hidden within him. This does not mean, of course, that he should act out his dark side and give free rein to all his repressions, a charge which the unenlightened public so often lay at the door of the psychotherapist. The acceptance of the shadow is not a *carte blanche* for licentiousness,[8] not a declaration of irresponsibility and a denial of self-determination. For why should consciousness, and the "free will" which is available only to consciousness, have been given to us, if it did not want us to make further use of its power?

Since the psyche is built on polar opposites which complement each other, but also stand in glaring contradiction to each other, it must of its very nature exist in a state of tension and suffer this. One can even say that the confrontation with these opposites lies at the heart of the individuation process. For this reason the suspension on the cross is such an excellent symbol for the authentic being of man. Hence the Christian summons to an *imitatio* of the crucified Christ touches on the deepest chord in our human nature. Usually, however, the *imitatio Christi* is understood and aspired to exclusively as an imitation of his divine perfection, but not of his tragic human fate, of his suffering and sacrifice. The four beams of the cross stretching in different directions point to a fundamental conflict and a corresponding state of torment, but their point of intersection, the centre of the cross, symbolizes the possibility of a union of opposites, to strive for which is likewise man's task. This characterizes the ambivalence which is the lot of man and which is so difficult to master.

For each of us would like to live only in a straight line, to have only one meaning, and not to be torn between our own inner contradictions. The fact that these cannot always be overcome, that not all of them can be cancelled out or neutralized, is a lesson which we learn in the course of life only through a long chain of experiences. But this exempts us neither from having to endure them nor from seeking to reconcile them. To be "whole" means, at the same time: to be full of contradictions. We falsify man when we try to sketch a homogeneous picture of him. The picture is true to life only when it is ambiguous and paradoxical. That is why it is so difficult to give an adequate description of him and of his psyche, and to relate oneself to his wholeness. One of the most valuable insights and conclusions conveyed by the individuation process is that paradox is an essential feature of human existence and of the psyche, and that one must learn to accept it and live with it.

The Christian knows that man is good and evil and that this antinomy is a fundamental characteristic of his psychic make-up. What else is meant by saying that we are all tainted with original sin? As soon as the light of consciousness dawned in man, as soon as he came to know his difference from God, he was exposed to the torment of opposites in his soul. For "only unconsciousness makes no difference between good and evil".[9] By eating of the tree of knowledge despite God's prohibition, his eyes were opened,[10] and they have remained open ever since, and presumably always will be. Painful and difficult as human existence became for ever afterward, being placed between good and evil is precisely the hallmark of man as man. Were it not so, he would not be able to discriminate, the opposites would not be separated, and everything would melt into everything else. "We must not overlook the fact that opposites acquire their moral accentuation only within the sphere of human endeavour and action, and that we are unable to give a definition of good and evil that could be considered universally valid. In other words, we do not know what good and evil are in themselves. It must therefore be supposed that they spring from a need of human consciousness and that for this reason they lose their validity outside the human sphere." [11]

If evil did not exist, man would perhaps not be able to discern the good. It is only through the intensity of the darkness that the light becomes visible in its full radiance. Only light *and* darkness make *one* day;[12] only good and evil make *one* man. Therefore Jung rightly says: "To confront a person with his shadow is to show him his own light . . . Anyone who perceives his shadow and his light simultaneously sees himself from two sides and thus gets in the middle." "He knows that the world consists of darkness and light. I can master their polarity only by freeing myself from them by contemplating both, and so reaching a middle position. Only there am I no longer at the mercy of the opposites." [13] And elsewhere he says: "In this world good and evil more or less balance each other, like day and night, and this is the reason why the victory of the good is always a special act of grace." [14]

Jung could never admit that evil, even in its most harmless aspect, is merely a "diminution" of good. He vehemently rejected the Catholic doctrine of evil as a *privatio boni*. The daily experienced reality of evil, its apparently ineradicable presence in our midst, its undeniable power were proof for Jung that it is a reality in itself, formidable and often ungovernable, which could not be denied an absolute value. No argument to the contrary could induce him to change his view, whose rightness he passionately defended in many of his writings.[15] At the same time he emphasized that he contested the validity of the *privatio boni* only in the empirical realm, expressly stating: "My attitude to this problem is empirical, not theoretical or aprioristic." [16] For "in the metaphysical realm . . . good may be a substance and evil non-existent (μὴ ὄν)",[17] but in actual experience it is otherwise. In other words, these two very different realms should not be confused with one another, as unfortunately often happens, particularly in theological circles. Rather, care should be taken to keep them rigorously apart.

In the human realm of experience, therefore, evil as much as good has a reality with which we are daily confronted. Anyone who evades this confrontation remains one-sided. As Pascal trenchantly remarks: "Man is neither angel nor brute, and the unfortunate thing is that he who would act the angel acts the brute." [18] And again: "It is dangerous to show man too clearly how much he resembles the beasts without at the same time showing him his greatness. It is also dangerous to allow him too clear a vision of his greatness without his baseness. It is even more dangerous to leave him in ignorance of both. But it is very profitable to show him both." [19] Words that exactly agree with the facts Jung has encountered in his practical work.

Absolute good and absolute evil no doubt exist as abstract concepts. But as soon as we consider them as psychological phenomena, we have to begin by asking: Which man, under what physical, social, and psychological conditions, has done, said, or thought such-and-such? Moreover, whether a thing is described as evil is largely dependent on a subjective judgment, as is the case also with the degree and gravity of a man's guilt. Let us consider, for example, the fifth commandment: "Thou shalt not kill." [20] Killing is undoubtedly a sin, but even it can be judged from different standpoints. It makes a difference whether a man kills out of cupidity, jealousy, or for revenge, or whether a mother, to save her child, kills its attacker, or whether a soldier kills an enemy as a patriotic duty.[21] Armies going into battle are even blessed by their churches; often it is the same church that blesses the soldiers of the opposing army. If a man is decorated for killing a particularly large number of the enemy in time of war, but is locked up in time of peace for killing a single individual—perhaps in self-defence—then it is not surprising that people are disoriented and that good and evil seem inextricably intermixed.

It is the same with the fourth commandment: "Honour thy

father and thy mother, that thy days may be long upon the land which the Lord thy God giveth thee." [22] The principle here expressed in abstract form can be followed in a great variety of ways in everyday reality. Some think they are "honouring" their parents best by remaining with them unmarried till their death; others, by marrying, founding a family, fostering their inheritance, and passing it on to their children; others, by emigrating to a distant country and building up a fortune that redounds to the good of their parents too. One man thinks he must be kind and polite to his parents at the cost of sincerity, another that a rough word and brusque behaviour are permissible if they come from a good heart. The way in which the commandment is obeyed will depend on the attitude, feeling, and judgment of the person in question, and each will be convinced that he has interpreted and applied the Biblical injunction correctly.

Most commandments and prohibitions lose their unequivocal meaning as soon as they are seen in a psychological light. What is forbidden and evil in one context may be permitted and good in another. Often it cannot be decided until afterwards whether what one has done was good or bad, right or wrong. So it is unavoidable that one occasionally takes a false step or lands oneself in conflicts. Moreover there are kinds of "guilt" and kinds of conflict of the subtlest nature, which begin where the law books leave off and remain inaccessible to even the deepest delving psychology. With such cases in mind, Jung says: "To see into the ultimate depths of the conviction behind the action is possible only to God." [23] Here we come to that border territory which sets a bound to our knowledge.

The dialectical discussion between the conscious contents and those coming from the unconscious realm of the psyche in the analytically assisted individuation process is at the same time a discussion between spirit and nature, the great pair of opposites in the psyche. It frequently acquires a moral accent, since good is identified with spirit and evil with nature. Jung was from the beginning passionately concerned with this problem, returning to it again and again till the end of his life. I shall therefore quote some of his statements on this theme from his autobiography:

"Evil has become a determinant reality. It can no longer be dismissed from the world by circumlocution. We must learn how to handle it, since it is here to stay. How we can live with it without terrible consequences cannot for the present be conceived.[24]

". . . Touching evil brings with it the grave peril of succumbing to it. We must, therefore, no longer succumb to anything at all, not even to good. A so-called good to which we succumb loses its ethical character. Not that there is anything bad in it on that score, but to have succumbed to it may breed trouble. Every form of addiction is bad, no matter whether the narcotic be alcohol or morphine or idealism. We must beware of thinking of good and evil as absolute opposites . . . Recognition of the reality of evil necessarily relativizes the good, and the evil likewise, converting both into halves of a paradoxical whole.

"In practical terms, this means that good and evil are no longer so self-evident. We have to realize that each represents a *judgment*. In view of the fallibility of all human judgment, we cannot believe that we will always judge rightly. We might so easily be the victims of misjudgment. The ethical problem is affected by this principle only to the extent that we become somewhat uncertain about the moral evaluations. *Nevertheless we have to make ethical decisions.*[25] The relativity of 'good' and 'evil' by no means signifies that these categories are invalid, or do not exist . . . I have pointed out many times that as in the past, so in the future the wrong we have done, thought, or intended will wreak its vengeance on our souls . . . Moral evaluation is always founded upon the apparent certitudes of a moral code which pretends to know precisely what is good and what evil. But once we know how uncertain the foundation is, ethical decision becomes a subjective, creative act. We

can convince ourselves of its validity only *Deo concedente*—
that is, there must be a spontaneous and decisive impulse on
the part of the unconscious.[26] Ethics itself, the decision between good and evil, is not affected by this impulse, only made
more difficult for us. Nothing can spare us the torment of
ethical decision . . .

"Therefore the individual who wishes to have an answer to
the problem of evil, as it is posed today, has need, first and
foremost, of *self-knowledge,* that is, the utmost possible knowledge of his own wholeness. He must know relentlessly how
much good he can do, and what crimes he is capable of, and
must beware of regarding the one as real and the other as illu-
sion. Both are elements within his nature, and both are bound
to come to light in him, should he wish—as he ought—to live
without self-deception or self-delusion." [27]

These statements and others like them, based on empirical
psychology, have earned Jung many critics and enemies, particularly among theologians. They protest that his relativiza-
tion of good and evil would destroy the moral values for man,
who, in his existential uncertainty, needs the guidance of unequivocal principles. With that Jung would largely agree, so
far as concerns all those who go the "natural" way of individuation, although even in these cases any one-sidedness, any abso-
lutization of behaviour or judgment leads to psychic difficulties. Jung would emphasize, however, that the analytically
guided individuation process with its problems, dangers, and
trials can and should be undertaken only by those who are
ready to accept all the risks and consequences of an ethical
conflict. Actually they have no choice, because it is simply their
destiny to face it consciously. The urge for self-realization, i.e.,
for the development of the personality, is inherent in every
man from the beginning.[28] Unless it is prematurely inhibited,
frustrated, or deflected,[29] it will drive him towards wholeness
and subject him to an individuation process whose most highly
developed "natural" form can equal or come very close to the
analytically guided one.

What is meant, then, is neither a wilful acting out nor a conscious denial of evil, but an admission that no human life can entirely escape it. We make convulsive efforts to keep only the good, the permitted thoughts and feelings in our consciousness, and to exclude the numerous drives and qualities which belong to our "non-angelic" side, which we do not want to admit even to ourselves, much less to others. Hence the rigid façade, the panic fear and aggressive self-defence whenever the slightest criticism puts our allegedly angelic side in question. To know that evil ever dwells within us, to learn to bear this knowledge instead of foisting it off on other people and always blaming them for everything, is one of the most important postulates of individuation.

The more the originally unconscious components of the personality, even the "evillest" of them, can be articulated with consciousness and kept in mind, the more it is possible to avoid evil. This, however, only in modest recognition that evil as much as good belongs to our human nature, and that it can also become that *felix culpa*[30] from whose darkness the light is born. For everything repressed, inferior, immoral, even pathological can, God willing, become the matrix for a renewal, for a rebirth on a higher level. In the negative and evil may be hidden the germs of a transformation into the positive and good; they can be the starting point for a reversal and purification. Not for nothing did William Blake picture the devilish Lucifer as a radiantly beautiful angel, for his name means "light-bringer".

Continually to avoid the encounter with evil, to live in perpetual fear of it, leads eventually to neurosis. Because of this fear, countless neurotics try desperately to "think out" life, to live it in imagination instead of experiencing it, closing their eyes to the existence of evil, above all in themselves. For only what is experienced affords certainty and security and becomes binding for the one who has had the experience. Hence it is necessary for the neurotic in particular to broaden his personality by venturing into life, to throw off his chains by expanding the field of consciousness, and therefore he is driven into

analysis just as strongly as he fears it. For his neurosis is perhaps a final call to individuation, to explore the blocked and
repressed possibilities lying fallow in him.

The "completeness" or "wholeness" of the personality
should never be confused with "perfection" in the moral or
religious sense. The former is a psychological goal, the aim being psychic balance and health, wisdom and tolerance, and
thus inner peace. It is directed to earthly life, is experienceable
here and now, and is more or less attainable. Perfection, on the
other hand, is the ideal goal of the Christian creeds, according
to which all earthly life, being but a passage to the Beyond,
must aim at this highest virtue, so that its ultimate realization
lies beyond all psychological endeavour, in the realm of faith
and religious truth. Any psychological endeavour, therefore,
even of the Jungian kind, is considered unsatisfactory from the
theological point of view, for according to Christ "there be
eunuchs which have made themselves eunuchs[31] for the kingdom of heaven's sake".[32] In psychological terms, that means:
those who have sacrificed their wholeness and completeness for
the sake of longed-for perfection. The goal of life would, in
theological language, be heaven, God, and not wholeness and
completeness of the personality. And yet, from the psychological standpoint one could reply: properly interpreted and experienced, the two points of view and their respective aims should
in no way exclude one another, but complement one another.

By way of substantiating this statement let us again draw on
the Bible, where we read: ". . . for he [your Father] maketh
his sun to rise on the evil and on the good, and sendeth rain on
the just and on the unjust . . . Be ye therefore perfect, even
as your Father which is in heaven is perfect." [33] Christ, therefore, postulates a "perfection" which, like God, embraces all
polarities of being. From whichever side one approaches them,
the religious or the psychological, the result would be the
same: inner peace.

This brings us to the problem of a *Weltanschauung*, a philosophy of life, which in Jung's view can be freely constructed

only by the man who has learnt to distinguish between what has been drummed into him and what he has acquired by his own experience and knowledge. "To have a *Weltanschauung* means to create a picture of the world and of oneself, to know what the world is and who I am . . . *cum grano salis*, it means the best possible knowledge—a knowledge that esteems wisdom and abhors unfounded assumptions, arbitrary assertions, and didactic opinions. Such knowledge seeks the well-founded hypothesis, without forgetting that all knowledge is limited and subject to error." [34] For "the world exists not merely in itself, but also as it appears to me".[35] Only the very few have a knowing faith, only the very few a philosophy of life won by insight and free choice, and based on a radical coming to grips with the problem of opposites in the psyche. Mostly our ego is a mere plaything, tossed between the unknown forces of the outer and inner worlds. A great deal is won, and much evil avoided, when we know something about the contents in our unconscious depths which are liable to assail us and lead us into temptation. Only thus are we armed against the autonomy and demonism that cling to everything unconscious and unknown.

Most people think that everything they do or omit to do is prompted by their conscious ego. They forget, or do not know, all the things that are alive and active in the psyche besides the ego, and that go on autonomously, without the participation of consciousness. They believe they know themselves perfectly and that their ego can rule in them as it pleases. To the question "Who am I?" or rather, "Who am I besides what I know of myself?" the individuation process seeks to give an answer. This answer will then largely decide the nature of one's *Weltanschauung*.

To many people it seems inconceivable that there could be in their psyche autonomous contents and an activity which is not "done" or "willed" by them. It is one of the most important achievements of the individuation process to experience this non-ego, to make it conscious to a large extent and to accept it as a helpful, constant companion. To live only within the lim-

ited confines of the ego is senseless and painful. But to participate knowingly in the boundless creative life of the psyche and
in the archetypal images of the non-ego is full of meaning, because whatever we do or omit to do is then resolved in something greater than the ego. Here a bridge may be thrown across
to the metaphysical realm, and here Jung's belief in God re-
veals itself. He asks: "The decisive question for man is: Are
you related to something infinite or not? That is the criterion
of his life . . . Only consciousness of our narrow confinement
in the self forms the link to the limitlessness of the unconscious.
In this consciousness we experience ourselves concurrently as
limited and eternal, as both the one and the other. In knowing
ourselves to be unique in our personal combination—that is,
ultimately limited—we possess also the capacity for becoming
conscious of the infinite." [36] Knowing participation in the "infinite" follows, in the psychological realm, from the awareness
of the inner God-image, of the Self.[37]

Intimations of heaven and hell have been man's since the
earliest times, for these are the two poles—the light and the
dark—between which his soul swings. A swing towards one
side is always followed by an equal swing towards the other.[38]
Peace is found *only at the centre,* where man can be wholly
man, neither angel nor devil, but simply man, partaker of both
worlds. The search for this centre, for this balance of the soul,
is a lifelong undertaking. It is the basic task and the ultimate
goal of psychotherapy. For this centre is also the place where
the Divine filters through into the soul and reveals itself in the
God-images, in the Self. It represents the moment of quies-
cence when the image of God can be perceived in the polished
mirror of the soul.

The "balance" meant here has nothing to do with what we
call "happiness" in the ordinary sense of the word, nor with
that state of freedom from care, suffering, and effort which hov-
ers before most people's eyes as the goal of their heart's desire.[39] Rather, it means a state in which both worlds, the light
and the dark, the good and the bad, the joyful and the sorrow-

ful, are united in self-evident acceptance and reflect the true nature of man, his inborn duality. In this sense the individuation process leads to the highest possible development and completeness of the psychic personality and is a preparation for the end of life.

Whether one goes the "natural", more or less unconscious way of individuation or takes the consciously worked through way depends, presumably, on fate. But one thing is certain: unconsciousness or wanting to remain unconscious, to escape the call to development and avoid the venture of life, is sin. For though growing old is the inescapable lot of all creatures, growing old meaningfully is a task ordained for man alone. What meaning has our life? None but what *we* give it.

Conclusion

THE consciously undertaken way of individuation can, as we have seen, be considered from several points of view. In conclusion, we will list some of the most important.

As a process of *psychological development,* it represents the step-by-step maturation of the human psyche to the point where all its potentialities are unfolded, and the conscious and unconscious realms are united by integrating its historical roots with present-day consciousness.

From the point of view of *characterology,* it throws the typological profile of the individual into ever clearer relief. It facilitates increasing control of the auxiliary functions and of the undeveloped, inferior function and attitude, resulting in a growing capacity for judgment and decision and an extension of the freedom of the will.

From the *sociological* point of view, it integrates the individual with the collective and adapts the ego to the demands of life.

In *psychotherapy* it brings about a redistribution of psychic energy, assists the dissolution of complexes, identifications, and fixations, as well as the withdrawal of projections. It furnishes a means of recognizing and enduring one's own shadow-qualities, of finding one's own values, and thus of overcoming neurosis.

Finally, from the *religious* point of view, it creates a living relation between man and the suprapersonal and gives him his proper place in the order of the universe. Through the encounter with the contents of the unconscious realm of the psyche and their integration with consciousness it lays the foundations of an independent, personal philosophy of life which, depending on the individual, may also ally itself with a particular creed.

The individuation process, however, cannot be grasped in its deepest essence, for it is a part of the mystery of transformation that pervades all creation. It includes within it the secret of life, which is ceaselessly reborn in passing through an ever renewed "death".

"If man is to live," says Jung, "he must fight and sacrifice his longing for the past in order to rise to his own heights. And having reached the noonday heights, he must sacrifice his love for his own achievement, for he may not loiter. The sun, too, sacrifices its greatest strength in order to hasten onward to the fruits of autumn, which are the seeds of rebirth." [1] If this sacrifice is made willingly—a deed possible for man alone and demanded again and again on the way of individuation—transformation and rebirth ensue.

Metaphorically, therefore, we could speak of the most important stations on the way of individuation as of four births.

The *first,* when the bodily man steps into life from the womb of his mother.

The *second,* at puberty, when the ego emancipates itself from its psychic fusion with the parental authority and acquires clearly defined form, independence, and sense of responsibility.

The *third,* when the "spiritual body" emerges from the conflicts of middle life and, anchored again in the depths of the psyche, man knowingly allies himself with the Self. Expressed in religious language, this experience is a "rebirth".

The *fourth,* when man departs through the door of life and re-enters the vast, unexplored land beyond death, from whence he came.

Most people, however, prefer to be born only once. They are

afraid of the pains without which there can be no birth. They have no trust in the natural striving of the psyche towards its goal. And so there are all too many who halt on life's way. They venture nothing, they would rather forgo the prize. Often even those who go the conscious way of individuation have not understood that the greatest problems in life can never be finally solved. "The meaning and purpose of a problem seem to lie not in its solution but in our working at it incessantly." [2]

These words of Jung's should console us for never having met a "fully individuated" person. For it is not the goal but the striving towards this goal that gives our life content and meaning.

Jolande Jacobi

This is a book about Jung's concept of individuation. It is also an account of how a remarkable psychotherapist sees her work. Like all good psychotherapy, this vision is personal. It has grown, active and passive, from the kaleidoscopic experience of European history in the last seventy years. To appreciate the quality of Dr. Jacobi's new book, it will help to know something about her life story and of the relationship in which she stands to Jung's work.

Lewis Mumford, in his fine review of Jung's autobiography, has emphasized how important it was for both Jung and Freud, in their personal struggle with the irrational, that they had an anchor not only in their families but also in "stability of residence in an identifiable historic city maintaining an orderly pattern of social relations that included many affectionate personal ties. No matter how far they might wander in their travels or in their minds, the continuity of their personalities was supported by the continuity of their homely urban environments."

Precisely this continuity was lacking for Jacobi. Twice in her life, political catastrophe destroyed her economic, social and familial environment. When aged thirty, and again at fifty, she had to create for herself a new life. She has never been able to forget that the quest for personal identity is not only a matter of inner definition. Man is wise, plays, uses tools. But also, and always, he is a political animal.

Jolande Székács was born in Budapest on 25 March 1890. Her father, senator and privy councillor to the Austro-Hungarian court, was a wealthy businessman engaged in the manufacture of glass. On her mother's side, one great uncle had been Deputy in the parliament at Warsaw, while another was professor of Mathematics at the University of Cracow. Both parents were of Jewish ancestry, but had been baptized as adults.

In Budapest, as elsewhere in Europe, the emancipation of women was one of the topical issues in the early years of the new century. Jolande's parents believed that the proper place of a woman was in the home, and it was only after a struggle that she obtained permission to study at a gymnasium at the age of fourteen. At nineteen plans for her further education were shelved when she met and married Dr. Andrew Jacobi, a distinguished Budapest lawyer, fourteen years her senior. Two sons were born in the years following the marriage.

Jacobi's description of her life in Budapest during the 1914–18 war shows a society with little idea that a world was coming to an end. But with more intuition than others in her circle, she sensed how things were changing, and insisted on training as a secretary in order to help her husband. It was a friendship made while working for her secretarial diploma that enabled her to escape with her family to Vienna, after the communist seizure of power in Budapest under Béla Kun in March 1919.

This was the first great upheaval in her life. From now on, the family lived in Vienna, though after the collapse of the communist government in Hungary they were able to renew their contacts in Budapest. In 1924, Jolande's husband was ill for eight months with a severe depression. It was her first contact with such illness. She read widely in an attempt to understand what was happening to her husband. After his recovery, Dr. Andrew Jacobi moved back to Budapest to renew his legal practice. He lived from then on half in Budapest and half with his family in Vienna, where he wanted his sons to be educated.

In 1926 Jacobi came into contact with the Kulturbund, the Austrian cultural organization which was to play a central role in her life for the next twelve years. Her energy and initiative soon led to her election as executive vice-president, and in this capacity she was soon at the centre of the cultural life of the Austrian capital, and in touch with many of the great names of Europe, men who in some cases became personal friends. In 1935 she was decorated with the Ritterkreuz des Oesterreichischen Verdienstordens, a rare distinction for a woman. And many years later, in 1957, the Austrian Government conferred Austrian citizenship on her, in recognition of her contribution to the cultural life of the republic during this period.

It was through the Kulturbund that she first met Jung and his wife in 1927, when he lectured in Vienna. She gave a luncheon party for the Swiss visitors at her apartment.

"At 4:30 the guests went, but Jung stayed to tell me about the *I Ching*. We sat on the floor and he showed me how to throw the coins. I still have the piece of paper, on which he wrote out from memory the 64 hexagrams. Until that day, I'd never heard of him. I didn't even know he existed. The whole afternoon he talked to me about 'the unconscious,' and how what we threw in the *I Ching* was so to say parallel with what was constellated within us."

In the following year, Jolande had the dream which is retold on page 76 of this book, a dream which in a sense gives the pattern of her life and of her own conception of psychotherapy. She sent it to Jung in Zurich, and he answered: "Now you are caught. Now you cannot get away."

The year before she met Jung, Jolande had become the friend of the Austrian writer Albert von Trentini. "I can truly say that it was Trentini who awakened my spirit and most deeply formed it, even before Jung," she says. From 1930 to 1933 Trentini was dying of cancer. His physical and religious suffering during those years had a decisive effect on Jacobi. She shared them with him and began herself to struggle more and more with problems of a religious character. She was present when Trentini received extreme unction and was so shaken and impressed that she decided to search deeper into the meaning of the Catholic faith, to understand better the significance of Trentini's struggles. Thus she became a Catholic herself, and was received into the Church a year after his death.

After Hitler came to power in Germany, she decided to write to Jung asking if he would train her as an analyst. He replied: only if she took a doctorate first. So, at the age of forty-four, she enrolled in 1934 at the University of Vienna, to study psychology under Karl and Charlotte Bühler. Since the experience of her husband's depression eleven years before, Jacobi had gained some personal knowledge of the various psychological schools active in Vienna. She had done a year's Adlerian analysis with Rudolf Dreikurs, and also worked for eighteen months with a Freudian—"not long enough for a proper analysis, but it gave me some insight into Freudian methods." (Her only meeting with Freud was at a birthday party in his honour, when she shook hands with him.) Through her friendship with Ernst Kris, then the editor of *Imago,* she had access to psychoanalytical circles, though never belonging to them.

She was still four months from completion of her doctorate when the Nazis occupied Austria in March 1938. She was in danger on account of her role in the Kulturbund, and after her flat had been ransacked by the Gestapo, she returned with her husband to Budapest. From there she wrote to Jung that under the circumstances she could not complete her studies, and proposing to come at once to Zurich. He replied: "I'm sorry. Don't come without a doctorate, I won't accept you for training." So she returned to Vienna. Avoiding her own flat, she stayed with a friend of her son, wore mourning to justify a veil, and, literally under the eyes of the Gestapo, took her Ph.D. with a dissertation on the Psychology of the Change of Life. Immediately afterwards, she returned to Budapest and finally, on 17 October 1938, came to Zurich. She was nearly forty-nine.

From 1938 to the present day, Jacobi's life has been inextricably involved with the work of Jung. But to understand the quality of this involvement, and therefore to appreciate the blend of what is Jung and what is Jacobi in this book, it is necessary to remember the range and intensity of her life before she moved to Zurich. She came to work under Jung not as a patient, but as a woman who had already asserted her independence in the areas of religion and feeling.

A recurring theme in this book is the distinction between the second and the first halves of life. Jacobi sees her own life as divided into three stages, Budapest, Vienna and Zurich. When she moved to Zurich, the development begun nineteen years earlier was taken a stage further. Much of her past identity was to be stripped from her. Only gradually did the new woman emerge.

When Jacobi first came to live in Switzerland, one son was already studying there. The elder son had completed his education and taken a job in Budapest. When the Nazis finally moved into Hungary in 1944, her father and mother committed suicide after their arrest by the Gestapo, and her husband died on the way to a concentration camp. It is with reference to this tragedy that she says: "I owe Jung my life." Only in 1956 could her elder son leave Hungary with his family, and join her in Switzerland.

Meanwhile, alone in Zurich in the early years of the war she found herself rejected by many Jews who regarded her as a double traitor to her people: through her parents' baptism, and through her own conversion to Catholicism; while as someone with Jewish ancestors, as a woman who had left her husband, as a foreigner with no money, there were people who felt it wiser to keep their distance. During this period, her membership of the Catholic Church, of a spiritual community extending beyond the borders of neutral but beleaguered Switzerland, gave her a sense of "belonging", of security.

But this erosion of her former identity served to stimulate enduring creative activity in the new field of psychology. The great dream of twelve years before was becoming reality. Already at Christmas 1938 on a visit to Budapest she had been invited to lecture on Jung's work to a small group. These lectures she later worked up into a slim volume which was published in German in 1940. (The English translation, *The Psychology of C. G. Jung*, appeared in 1942, in London and New York, and has since gone through six editions.) Jung consented to write a forword. This contribution to Jacobi's book resulted in the banning of his own books throughout Nazi occupied Europe.

This first book was followed in 1941 by her study of Paracelsus, and for Jung's seventieth birthday in 1945 she published a large anthology from his works, *Psychological Reflections*. A further major work of exposition, *Complex/Archetype/Symbol,* appeared in 1956. She has also published over eighty articles, and is now working on two further full-length studies, on the psychology of women and on the interpretation of paintings in psychotherapy.

After the war, other fields were opened to her initiative. She played a leading part in the founding of the C. G. Jung Institute in Zurich in 1948. She began to lecture frequently at various universities in Switzerland, and later in London, Paris, Amsterdam, Leyden, The Hague, Munich, Stuttgart, Berlin, Vienna. In the winter of 1953 to 1954 she visited the United States, and gave over fifty lectures, including three courses at the New School for Social Research in New York, and at Yale, Princeton, Harvard, Baltimore, San Francisco, and Los Angeles.

But behind her writing and her teaching has been the growth of her international practice as psychotherapist. This has been the seedbed from which her books and lectures have grown, and the laboratory in which she has used the formulas of Jung's psychology to achieve in her own life the marriage of extraversion and introversion that provides the leitmotif of this book.

Few of Jung's concepts have acquired such a wide circulation, and been so debased in the process, as "extravert" and "introvert." Within the existing corpus of writing on Jung's psychology, Jacobi's natural acceptance of the value of the extraverted way has assured her books a wide public. But for those who have worked with her, the precious balance she has achieved between outer and inner worlds has come to mean something very personal. She has brought to the inward probing analysis of much contemporary psychotherapy a strong breath of the Homeric view of human nature as something "outward and discrete and centrifugal, a continuous dying into the full life of the self through the self's dissipation in action." It is the tension between this centrifugal vision and the introversion associated with Jung's later work that gives to her life today its extraordinarily vivid quality, wounded yet inviolate.

DAVID HOLT

NOTES

The Forerunners

1) C. G. Carus, *Psyche,* p. x. In his *Psychologie* (1808) Carus had already treated the problem of the human life-span and its different phases and anticipated many present-day theories.

2) For example, the painting of the three kings attributed to the Oberrheinischer Meister, ca. 1400, Kunsthalle, Hamburg. Similar paintings by numerous medieval masters may be found in practically all the great museums.

3) Francis Howard Collection, London.

4) Hesiod, according to Agricola, maxim 661. (Transl.: Evelyn-White, Loeb Classics, London, New York, 1920.)

5) Psalm 90:10 (RSV).

6) This theme is frequently depicted in the engravings of earlier centuries. One example is the fine engraving by Jörg Breu d. J., ca. 1530 (see frontispiece).

7) W. Grimm, *Tierfabeln bei den Meistersingern,* p. 248.

8) La Rochefoucauld, *Reflections ou sentences et maximes morales.* Paris, 1838. *The Moral Maxims and Reflections of the Duke de la Rochefoucauld,* by G. H. Powell, London.

9) Charlotte Bühler, *Der menschliche Lebenslauf als psychologisches Problem.*

10) *Ibid.,* p. 68.

11) It is at the end of this phase that the "change of life" usually occurs.

12) Cf. also A. L. Vischer, *Das Alter als Schicksal und Erfüllung,* esp. p. 52.

13) By "depth psychology" is meant all trends in psychology and psychotherapy which, in their theoretical conceptions and their prac-

tical, medical work, take account of the "unconscious", i.e., a psychic realm neither known nor controlled by the conscious mind. Cf. *infra,* n. 5 of "Individuation".

Individuation

1) *Psychiatric Studies* (Collected Works, vol. 1), p. 79.

2) H. Schmidt, *Philosophisches Wörterbuch,* p. 294.

3) R. Eisler (*Handwörterbuch der Philosophie,* p. 308) defines individuation as the "differentiation of the general, of species into singulars, of existence into a multiplicity of individuals". The *principium* is the factor that determines individuality. According to Aristotle (384–322 B.C.), Avicenna (980–1037), Albertus Magnus (1207–1280), and others, this factor lies in matter.

✓ The cause of individuation is sometimes located in form, sometimes in matter, sometimes in the union of the two, sometimes in the intellect, the will, or the instincts of organisms that assert and maintain themselves as individual beings. Individuation is itself original, or arose from something originally homogeneous (by emanation, evolution, differentiation, deterioration, etc.). (Eisler, *Wörterbuch der philosophischen Begriffe und Ausdrücke,* I, pp. 566 ff.)

According to Thomas Aquinas (1225–1274), matter is *"signata vel individualis"*; according to the nominalists, e.g., William of Occam (1290–1349), Leibniz (1646–1716), "the real is of itself individual: *quaelibet res singularis se ipsa est singularis"*. According to Spinoza (1632–1677), individuation is the determination of the general, a limitation of the One Being. According to Meister Eckhart (1260–1377), the principle of individuation lies in the temporal-spatial determination of the *hic et nunc.* John Locke (1632–1704) says it is "existence itself, which determines a being of any sort to a particular time and place, incommunicable to two beings of the same kind".

An intermediate position stresses the need for the collaboration of individuals, of great personalities and the mass. Thus W. Wundt (1832–1920) says: "Everywhere the individual is sustained by the collective mind, in which he participates with all his thoughts, feelings, desires. But in the leading minds . . . the whole process of past development condenses to produce effects which now point out new paths for the collective mind" (*Ethik,* pp. 491, 458 ff.). According to Schopenhauer (1788–1860), time and space, which are only subjective forms of perception, are the reason why the one "will", the "thing-in-itself", appears as a multiplicity of individuals.

4) By "psychic wholeness" Jung understands a unity based on the complementary interplay of the various aspects of the psyche (above all, of its conscious and unconscious realms), which is more than the sum of its parts. It represents the best possible and most complete development and integration of the individual's psychic qualities.

5) " 'Capacity for consciousness' naturally presupposes consciousness and self-awareness. By self-awareness we mean the quality which the psyche possesses of being aware of its contents—a quality independent of its structure and not more closely definable. It can pass through all stages to the counterpole of relative or absolute unconciousness. The experience of sinking into sleep and waking out of it makes this familiar to everyone. The objective determination of the degree of consciousness at a given time, such as full luminosity, somnolence, stupor, coma, etc., particularly in the lighter stages of unconsciousness, is one of the most difficult tasks facing the investigator.

"Everything that in a given psyche up to a given time is characterized by self-awareness we call *conscious.* Everything, on the contrary, that is not characterized by self-awareness is *unconscious* . . . Much that is commonly called 'unconscious' in the literature of depth psychology is relatively, not absolutely, unconscious." (K. W. Bash, "Zur Psychologie akuter symptomatischer Psychosen", in *Der Nervenarzt,* May 1957, pp. 193 f.)

The Two Kinds of Individuation

1) "The Psychology of the Child Archetype", in *The Archetypes and the Collective Unconscious* (CW, Vol. 9, Part I), pp. 170 f.

2) "The Ages of Life", in *Essays from the Parerga and Paralipomena,* p. 113.

3) I am indebted to Prof. Franz Borbély for these observations.

4) Cf. Bühler, *Der menschliche Lebenslauf,* p. 271. Examples of both forms are given with biographical data. Another good example of a "completed short life" may be found in Otto Braun, *Aus nachgelassenen Schriften eines Frühvollendeten.*

5) Gerhard Adler, *Studies in Analytical Psychology,* p. 109.

6) There are people who think they can achieve by a kind of "self-analysis" the same result as those who submit themselves to an analytically conducted individuation process. This is an error, and a dangerous one. Nobody can see beyond himself; even Baron Münchhausen could not pull himself out of the bog by his own pigtail. Only an objective partner can help one to gain the right insights and hence genuine self-knowledge.

7) "On the Nature of the Psyche", in *The Structure and Dynamics of the Psyche* (CW, Vol. 8), p. 187.

The Two Main Phases
of the Individuation Process

1) "The Stages of Life", *ibid.,* p. 397.

2) O. Schwarz.

3) "The Stages of Life" (CW, Vol. 8), p. 402.

4), 5) These terms were coined by Charlotte Bühler.

6) *Two Essays on Analytical Psychology* (CW, Vol. 7), par. 114.

7) "Woman in Europe", in *Civilization in Transition* (CW, Vol. 10), p. 132.

8) Schopenhauer, *Essays from the Parerga and Paralipomena,* p. 102.

9) It is instructive that in a questionnaire I prepared for my doctoral thesis on the psychology of the change of life, and sent round to female subjects of about fifty, it turned out that the first problems relating to a diminution of sexual interest generally began at the age of forty-two. As there is statistical evidence that the menopause does not begin, on average, until the age of forty-seven or forty-eight, one must assume that the female psyche is prepared several years in advance for this fundamental change.

10) *The Inner World of Childhood.* In a still unpublished lecture Fordham has pointed out that a kind of individuation process can be found even in the small child if we follow its development from birth to about its second year. By developing out of a total identification with the surrounding world, the small child gains more and more consciousness. Since Jung states in *Psychological Types* (Definition 29) that "individuation is practically the same as the development of consciousness out of the original state of identity", and, as Fordham

says, "the range and nature of identifications differ in each stage of life", it can rightly be maintained that "the essentials of the individuation process start in infancy and continue throughout life". It can, however, only be the beginning of the "natural" individuation process which is inherent in all living organisms.

11) *The Life of Childhood.*

12) *Children and Their Religion.*

13) *Das Kind.*

14) Jacobi, "Jungs Beitrag zur Psychologie des Kindes", in *Der Psychologe*, Heft 10; "Das Kind wird ein Ich", *Heilpädogogische Werkblätter*, No. 3; "Ich und Selbst in der Kinderzeichnung", *Schweiz. Zeitschrift für Psychologie*, Heft 1; *Complex/Archetype/Symbol*, Part II: "Archetype and Dream", pp. 125 ff.

15) The fact that Jung sometimes applies the term "individuation process" to the whole course of life, and sometimes only to a task beginning with the second half, has, unfortunately, given rise to many misunderstandings and misinterpretations.

16) "Commentary on the *Secret of the Golden Flower*", in *Alchemical Studies* (CW, Vol. 13), par. 68.

17) "The Soul and Death", in *The Structure and Dynamics of the Psyche* (CW, Vol. 8), p. 407.

18) The essays are included in *The Development of Personality* (CW, Vol. 17).

19) Cf. "The Psychology of the Child Archetype", in *The Archetypes of the Collective Unconscious* (CW, Vol. 9, Part I), pp. 151 ff.

20) By *puer aeternus* Jung means primarily those "eternal youths", most of them badly mother-fixated individuals stuck on the level of puberty, who, filled with youthful ideals, are unable to adapt to reality. What is appropriate for them in youth, and endows them with vitality and spiritual verve, proves in later years to be an oppressive neurosis, often lasting till death. We find these figures in mythology as the "divine boys" who blossom early and die young, like the old Germanic god Baldur, or the gods of the Near East, Tammuz, Attis, Adonis. They also appear in literature, e.g., Euphorion in Goethe's *Faust*, the little prince in Saint-Exupéry's novel of that name, the boy Fo in Bruno Goetz's *Reich ohne Raum*, to give but a few examples. There are naturally also *puellae aeternae*, who are likewise unadapted. Academic women with the souls of romantic flappers are examples of such. When these figures appear in dreams they

always have a dual aspect, like genuine symbols: on the one hand they represent undeveloped, still adolescent psychic traits of which the dreamer should become conscious in order to develop, on the other they are anticipations of dormant possibilities in the psyche. In this sense they are heralds of possible growth and of a potential rebirth on a maturer level.

21) Jung distinguishes two "attitude types": the extravert, oriented to the outer world, and the introvert, oriented to his own inner world.

22) Besides the "attitude types" Jung distinguishes four "function types", according to whether thinking, feeling, sensation, or intuition is differentiated into the dominant function as a mode of apprehension. Cf. *Psychological Types* (trans. Baynes), also pp. 34 ff.

23) Cf. M.-L. von Franz's *Kommentar zu "Reich ohne Raum"*, in which she gives an excellent diagnosis of this type of man and of his effect on historical events.

24) "Psychology and Literature", in *The Spirit in Man, Art, and Literature* (CW, Vol. 15), par. 161.

25) *Ibid.*, par. 158.

26) "The Gifted Child", in *The Development of Personality* (CW, Vol. 17), p. 141.

27) *Ibid.*

28) "Analytical Psychology and Education", *ibid.*, p. 115.

29) Cf. "Synchronicity: An Acausal Connecting Principle", in *The Structure and Dynamics of the Psyche* (CW, Vol. 8), p. 447.

30) Liliane Frey-Rohn, "Die Anfänge der Tiefenpsychologie", in *Festschrift zu Jungs 80. Geburtstag*, I, p. 73.

31) Erich Neumann, "Die Psyche und die Wandlung der Wirklichkeitsebenen", *Eranos-Jahrbuch 1951.*

32) Just as Freud saw the psychic beginnings of the ego in the Id, which consists of a bundle of undifferentiated drives, so analytical psychology supposes that it is first of all contained in the Self, the central, ordering authority in the psyche, and grows out of it. Jung speaks of initial "islands of consciousness" (CW, Vol. 8, pp. 189 f.) which, later become a unity, constitute the ego. According to Fordham's theory, there are to begin with ego germs, ego particles, which get welded together into larger and larger units through experiential encounters with the surrounding world, but which "de-integrate" again, and then continually re-integrate until the ego has achieved a

relative stability and density with a corresponding extension. In cases of a "weak ego" this process has not come to a satisfactory conclusion; it has remained "unfinished". Fordham also explains the easy dissociability of an ego as a malfunctioning of this process. (Cf. Fordham, "On the Origins of the Ego in Childhood", *Studien zur Analytischen Psychologie*, I, p. 80.)

33) Hermann Hesse, *Demian,* p. 176.

34) *Memories, Dreams, Reflections,* ed. Aniela Jaffé, p. 127 (E. 127).

35) *Ibid.,* p. 110 (E. 112).

36) *Ouroboros* is a Greek word meaning "tail-eater", referring to the dragon that bites its own tail. Here it represents the circular snake, symbolizing eternal movement in a circle. Its origin is ascribed by Macrobius to the Phoenicians (Neumann, *The Origins and History of Consciousness*, p. 10). It can also be found in the oldest Greek texts on alchemy published by Berthelot (*Collection des anciens alchimistes grecs*). A symbol with many meanings, it stands on the one hand for the *prima materia,* and on the other for the "All", the "one world", the totality of beginning and end, and has many other meanings. Cf. Figs. 6, 46, and 147 in Jung, *Psychology and Alchemy* (CW, Vol. 12).

37) From a letter of Jung's to the author, 1945.

The Stages

1) See *infra,* p. 37.

2) "On the Nature of the Psyche" (CW, Vol. 8), pp. 207 f.

3) "Concerning Rebirth", in *The Archetypes of the Collective Unconscious* (CW, Vol. 9, Part I), p. 123.

4) Ulrich Zwingli, *De vera et falsa religione,* 1525.

5) Schiller, "The Veiled Image at Sais", *The Poems of Schiller,* London, 1901, p. 120.

6) *Aion* (CW, Vol. 9, Part II), p. 30.

7) "The Aims of Psychotherapy", in *The Practice of Psychotherapy* (CW, Vol. 16), p. 39.

8) *Memories, Dreams, Reflections,* pp. 196 f. (E. 188).

9) "Amplification" is the name given by Jung to a process in which one enriches a dream motif with as many parallels as possible from

other spheres of knowledge or culture, in order to work out its meaning. Jung distinguishes a subjective and an objective amplification: the first consists of the personal associations of the dreamer, the second of associations which may also be supplied by the analyst, comprising material of similar meaning drawn from, say, mythology and the history of symbolism. Unlike Freud's method of "free association", the associations are "directed" and always relate to the dream element.

10) *Memories, Dreams, Reflections,* p. 187 (E. 179).

11) Aniela Jaffé, "Der Tod des Vergil", *Studien zur Analytischen Psychologie,* II, p. 298.

12) The fact that everyone is physically and psychically bisexual was known in the earliest times, though mostly the bisexuality referred to the bodily constitution. There are numerous myths and legends representing androgyny as the original "unitary" mode of human existence. The hermaphrodite as a symbol of wholeness plays a great role in alchemy. Cf. Jung, "The Psychology of the Transference", ch. 10, in *The Practice of Psychotherapy* (CW, Vol. 16), also Plato's *Symposium* and Ovid's *Metamorphoses.* Further information in E. Hollander, *Wunder, Wundergeburt und Wundergestalt,* pp. 39 ff.

13) The concept of the "unconscious" is actually an impermissible hypostatization. Nevertheless, it has proved its value as a heuristic conception, for which reason Jung makes use of it whenever he wishes to designate the vast area of the psyche lying outside the field of consciousness. He distinguishes the "personal unconscious", whose contents are ontogenetically acquired, and the "collective unconscious", whose contents are derived from phylogenesis. These latter are specifically human, typical modes of action and reaction, irrepresentable propensities which he terms "archetypes". They become perceptible to consciousness under definite constellations in the form of archetypal images, symbols, or processes. On the one hand they are "reflections" of the instincts, on the other they express ideations. Hence Jung distinguishes between the non-perceptible archetype *per se* and the perceptible archetypal image. The ego is conditioned not only by the unconscious psyche but also very largely by the "collective consciousness". By this term Jung means the sum total of traditions, conventions, customs, prejudices, rules, and norms of the environment in which the individual lives, and the spirit of the age by which

he is influenced. Cf. Jacobi, *Complex/Archetype/Symbol*, pp. 110 ff.

14) "Commentary on the *Secret of the Golden Flower*", in *Alchemical Studies* (CW, Vol. 13), par. 17.

15) "Numinosity" is a kind of divine efficacy emanating from the *mysterium tremendum, fascinosum, sacrum*. The term was introduced into literature by Rudolf Otto in his book *The Idea of the Holy*.

16) *Psychology and Religion* (CW, Vol. 11), pp. 520 f.

17) Needless to say, the numinosity and profusion of this material vary with the individual. We know moreover that archetypal images are a regular phenomenon with people, artists for instance, whose psychic background is particularly rich in imagery and fantasy, and that their appearance is by no means confined to a particular phase of the individuation process. They often appear at times of sudden crisis, serious illness, erotic fascination, etc., i.e., usually when the alertness of consciousness is relaxed.

Ego and Self

1) "Transformation Symbolism in the Mass", *Psychology and Religion* (CW, Vol. 11), p. 259.

2) From a letter to the theologian Walter Bernet, autumn 1955.

3) *Psychology and Religion* (CW, Vol. 11), p. 261.

4) *Psychology and Alchemy* (CW, Vol. 12), par. 11.

5) *Ibid.*, par. 15.

6) "General Aspects of Dream Psychology", *The Structure and Dynamics of the Psyche* (CW, Vol. 8), p. 278.

7) *Two Essays on Analytical Psychology* (CW, Vol. 7), p. 70.

8) "Brother Klaus", *Psychology and Religion*, p. 320.

9) *Psychology and Alchemy*, par. 12.

10) *Ibid.*, par. 19.

11) Luke 17:21.

12) On the psychosomatic level the relation between ego and Self might be compared with that between the human brain and the solar plexus.

13) "Die Psyche und die Wandlung der Wirklichkeitsebenen", *Eranos-Jahrbuch 1951*, p. 211.

14) Aniela Jaffé, "Der Tod des Vergil", *Studien zur Analytischen Psychologie*, II, p. 333.

15) W. von Siebenthal, *Die Wissenschaft vom Traum*, p. 241.

16) *Aion* (CW, Vol. 9, Part II), p. 42.

17) A. Jung, in his review of R. Hostie, *C. G. Jung und die Religion*, in *Anima*, Heft 4, 1957, p. 374.

18) "A Psychological Approach to the Dogma of the Trinity", *Psychology and Religion* (CW, Vol. 11), p. 178.

19) Concerning the significance of the quaternity as a symbol of psychic wholeness, see, in particular, *Psychology and Religion*, *Psychology and Alchemy*, *Aion*, *Mysterium Coniunctionis*, index, "quaternity".

20) *Psychology and Religion*, p. 57.

21) *Psychology and Alchemy*, par. 22.

22) *Ibid.*, par. 18.

23) *Psychology and Religion*, pp. 81 f.

24) "Concerning Rebirth", *The Archetypes and the Collective Unconscious* (CW, Vol. 9, Part I), pp. 145 f.

25) Jung contrasts "active imagination" with "passive imagination". In passive imagination the ego simply lets the inner images unfold and pass by, as in day-dreaming. In active imagination it participates in the interior drama, but without interfering and judging. Cf. *Two Essays on Analytical Psychology* (CW, Vol. 7), pars. 343 ff.; "The Transcendent Function", *Structure and Dynamics of the Psyche* (CW, Vol. 8), pp. 82 ff.; *Mysterium Coniunctionis* (CW, Vol. 14), pp. 495 f., 528 f.

26) A Sanskrit term Jung took over from the realm of Eastern meditation. It can be translated as "magic circle". Cf. "A Study in the Process of Individuation" and "Concerning Mandala Symbolism" in *Archetypes and the Collective Unconscious*.

27) *Psychology and Alchemy*, par. 249.

28) It might be conjectured that the art of schizophrenics differs from that of so-called normal persons in that the Gestalt-making quality of the psyche, its capacity to create an orderly pattern, has been put out of action. Cf. F. Reitmann, *Psychotic Art*.

29) Cf. *The Structure and Dynamics of the Psyche*, pp. 67 ff.

30) "Commentary on the *Secret of the Golden Flower*", *Alchemical Studies* (CW, Vol. 13), par. 24.

The Archetype
of the Individuation Process

1) *Ibid.,* par. 4.

2) Cf. Neumann, *The Origins and History of Consciousness,* where this problem is discussed at great length.

3) "Concerning Rebirth," *The Archetypes and the Collective Unconscious,* p. 116.

4) *Ibid.*

5) In his essay Jung distinguishes five forms of rebirth: 1. Transmigration of souls, or metempsychosis, 2. Reincarnation, 3. Resurrection, or transformation of one's being, 4. Renewal of personality, 5. "Indirect rebirth" through participation in a process of transformation, e.g., a rite, in which the participant experiences his own psychological transformation and the transcendence of life.

6) There is a Gnostic myth according to which the spirit or mind, Nous, fell in love with matter, Physis, sank into her embrace, and had to be freed from his "imprisonment". Cf. A. J. Festugière, *La Révélation d'Hermes Trismegiste,* esp. Vol. III. Paris 1947.

7) In this sense Meister Eckhart says: "All cereal means wheat, all treasure means gold, all generation means man". "Sermons and Collations", XXIX, in *Works* (trans. Evans), Vol. I, p. 80.

8) "Concerning Rebirth", p. 115.

9) *Psychology and Alchemy,* Fig. 171. Cf. K. Kerényi, "Vater Helios", *Eranos-Jahrbuch 1943,* p. 81.

10) *Symbols of Transformation,* Fig. 24, p. 241.

11) Copious material on this theme in M. Eliade, *The Myth of the Eternal Return.* Cf. also C. Hentze, *Tod, Auferstehung und Weltordnung.*

12) Cf. *supra,* p. 18.

13) Cf. *supra,* pp. 21 ff.

14) Cf. *supra,* pp. 53 ff.

15) A further example is the bull slain by Mithras in the Mithraic mysteries, from whose body the "world" is produced. (Jung, *Symbols of Transformation,* CW, Vol. 5, p. 238.) Mithras is a sun-hero, and through the sacrifice of his instinctual side (the bull, which stands for the archaic monster) the world comes into being, i.e., conscious-

ness dawns. Cf. F. Cumont, *The Mysteries of Mithra,* and A. Dieterich, *A Mithraic Ritual.*

16) The journey to Hades, or descent into the land of the dead. "Nekyia" is the title of the 11th book of Homer's *Odyssey.* Cf. Dieterich, *Nekya,* pp. 26 f., H. Gunkel, *Schöpfung und Chaos in Urzeit und Endzeit,* and E. Smith, *The Evolution of the Dragon.*

17) The literature on this subject is so voluminous that the citation of particular works and authors must be abandoned. The theme is touched on here only so far as it permits an analogy with the individuation process.

18) The cause or purpose of initiations is open to various interpretations. Freud took them as a defence against the incest-wish which exists in all young people. The Basel ethnologist F. Speiser thought they guaranteed the transfer of "vital force" from one generation to another. (Speiser, *Ueber Initiationem in Australien und Neuguinea.*) For Jung the principle motif was the idea of a symbolic death followed by rebirth, a view widely held today.

19) Reference should be made here to the shamans, their mysticomagical powers, the symbolism of their ecstatic practices, and their significance in the history of religion, all documented fully by M. Eliade in his book *Shamanism: Archaic Techniques of Ecstasy.*

20) For the sake of comparison we might mention the custom, prevalent among some Christian orders, of giving a candidate for the priesthood a new name when he enters his novitiate. It sometimes happens, too, that a writer will give himself a new name in middle life. An example is Hermann Hesse, who published his novel *Demian,* written when he was forty-two, under the pseudonym Emil Sinclair.

21) In New Guinea, for example.

22) Cf. Eliade, *Birth and Rebirth,* and Speiser, *op. cit.* Also P. Radin, *Gott und Mensch in der primitiven Welt,* pp. 167 ff., and J. G. Frazer, *The Golden Bough* (abridged edn., 1924), pp. 693 ff.

23) Cf. Apuleius, *The Golden Ass.*

24) Cf. *Eranos-Jahrbuch 1939: Vorträge über die Symbolik der Wiedergeburt,* and *The Mysteries: Papers from the Eranos Yearbooks,* Vol. 2. An excellent summary of various rebirth mysteries may be found in Dieterich, *A Mithraic Ritual.*

25) E. Lennhoff, *Die Freimaurer.*

26) W. E. Peukert, *Die Rosenkreuzer.*

27) O. Casel, *Das christliche Kultusmysterium* and *Das christliche Festmysterium,* also H. Rahner, "The Christian Mystery and the Pagan Mysteries" in *The Mysteries,* pp. 337 ff.

28) Jung, "Transformation Symbolism in the Mass", *Psychology and Religion* (CW, Vol. 11), p. 220.

29) *Symbols of Transformation* (CW, Vol. 5), pp. 209 ff.

30) Frobenius, *Das Zeitalter des Sonnengottes.*

31) *Symbols of Transformation,* p. 210, reproduced from Frobenius, *op. cit.,* p. 59.

32) Cf. Jacobi, *Complex/Archetype/Symbol,* pp. 179 ff.

33) For details of the myth see Frazer, *The Golden Bough* (abridged edn., 1924), pp. 362 ff.

34) For a psychological interpretation of the Osiris myth see Neumann, *The Origins and History of Consciousness,* pp. 220 ff.

35) Cf. A. Avalon, *The Serpent Power,* and J. W. Hauer, *Seminar Notes on Tantra Yoga* (privately multigraphed by the Psychology Club, Zurich). All yoga techniques are actually an initiation into a higher, spiritual reality.

36) When Atman is realized, the individual ceases to exist as such. In psychological terms, the ego is replaced by the Self.

37) The existing literature on the *exercitia* is naturally written entirely from a theological or philosophical point of view. At present there is no psychological interpretation other than Jung's seminar *Exercitia Spiritualia of St. Ignatius of Loyola,* ETH-Notes, June 1939 to March 1940 (privately multigraphed by the C. G. Jung Institute, Zurich).

38) The Easter candle is plunged into the water of the font. Thus the "fire initiation" is followed by a "water initiation", which is at the same time a *coniunctio,* a union of opposites (fire and water).

39) The alchemists were the medieval forerunners of modern chemists, but partly also of psychologists. Originating in Egypt, alchemy reached the West ca. 1100 via the Arabs. Its heyday was the end of the Middle Ages, when many alchemists were already aware of the psychological and symbolic meaning of their experiments and made conscious use of it. Hence the bizarre, encoded language of many alchemical treatises.

40) For a detailed account see *Psychology and Alchemy* (CW, Vol. 12).

41) Cf. *supra,* pp. 35 f.

42) Cf. *supra,* pp. 43 f.

43) Cf. *supra,* p. 46.

44) Of the *lapis* Jung says in his *Mysterium Coniunctionis* that it stands for "total union".

45) The hardness of the alchemical "stone" has a parallel in the Indian *vajra.* Originally this was the weapon of the god Indra and was called the thunderbolt. Later it was equated with the diamond, the hardest and most durable of all stones. The diamond is also a symbol of the absolute. (I am indebted for this information to Dr. Paul Horsch.)

46) *The Dream of Poliphilo.*

47) *Journey into Self,* an interpretation of Bunyan's *Pilgrim's Progress.*

48) *Die Anima als Schicksalsproblem des Mannes.*

49) R. Woods, *The World of Dreams,* pp. 668 ff., and Jacobi, *Complex/Archetype/Symbol,* "The Dream of the Bad Animal", pp. 127 ff.

50) *Memories, Dreams, Reflections,* p. 206 (E. 197).

51) CW, Vol. 7.

52) With Richard Wilhelm, trans. Cary F. Baynes (revised edn., 1962). The "European Commentary" is contained in *Alchemical Studies* (CW, Vol. 13).

53) Contained in *Psychology and Religion: West and East* (CW, Vol. 11).

54) CW, Vol. 12.

55) Contained in *The Practice of Psychotherapy* (CW, Vol. 16).

56) CW, Vol. 9, Part II.

57) CW, Vol. 14.

58) Basic material relating to this sphere of problems may also be found in the writings of Leo Frobenius, Heinrich Zimmer, Karl Kerényi, Mircea Eliade, Henri Corbin, etc.

The Individual Way

1) Schopenhauer, *Essays from the Parerga and Paralipomena,* p. 55 and n. 2.

2) *Two Essays on Analytical Psychology* (CW, Vol. 7), par. 266.

3) "The Meaning of Psychology for Modern Man", in *Civilization in Transition* (CW, Vol. 10), p. 149.

4) "The Undiscovered Self", *ibid.*, p. 291.

5) *Ibid.*, p. 254.

6) *Two Essays on Analytical Psychology*, par. 198.

7) *The Development of Personality* (CW, Vol. 17), p. 171.

8) "On the Nature of the Psyche", *Structure and Dynamics of the Psyche* (CW, Vol. 8), pp. 225 f.

9) This concept is central to the school of psychotherapy founded by Harry Stack Sullivan (U.S.A.).

10) *Psychology and Religion* (CW, Vol. 11), p. 89.

11) *The Development of Personality*, p. 173.

12) "On the Nature of the Psyche", p. 226.

13) *Psychological Types* (CW, Vol. 6), Definition 29.

14) *Memories, Dreams, Reflections*, p. 356 (E. 328).

15) *Mysterium Coniunctionis* (CW, Vol. 14), pp. 468 f.

16) *The Development of Personality*, p. 171.

17) The various aspects of the tree symbol are discussed by Jung in "The Philosophical Tree", *Alchemical Studies* (CW, Vol. 13).

Conscious Realization

1) *Memories, Dreams, Reflections*, p. 212 (E. 300).

2) Archetypal dreams can often be observed in children. As their ego is not yet fully formed and is easily swamped by the contents of the unconscious, children live in a state of fusion with the world of archetypal and mythological images. This would explain their love and intuitive understanding of fairytales and legends, which always represent archetypal modes of behaviour.

3) Cf. *supra*. p. 59.

4) Cf. *supra*, p. 31.

5) Cf. Liliane Frey-Rohn, "Die Anfänge der Tiefenpsychologie", *Studien zur Analytischen Psychologie*, I, p. 73.

6) Cf. Jung, "The Psychology of the Transference", in *The Practice of Psychotherapy* (CW, Vol. 16).

7) *Memories, Dreams, Reflections*, p. 212 (E. 203).

8) Compare in *Mysterium Coniunctionis* (CW, Vol. 14), p. 419, n. 211.

9) Cf. *supra,* p. 18.

10) It applies only to Freud's view of the unconscious.

11) "On Psychic Energy", in *The Structure and Dynamics of the Psyche* (CW, Vol. 8), p. 59.

12) Preface to *Seelenprobleme der Gegenwart,* p. v.

13) Jung often called the realm of the collective unconscious the "non-ego".

14) Cf. *supra,* p. 68.

15) *Memories, Dreams, Reflections,* p. 317 (E. 293).

16) "Commentary on the *Secret of the Golden Flower*", *Alchemical Studies* (CW, Vol. 13), par. 18.

17) "The Stages of Life", *Structure and Dynamics of the Psyche* (CW, Vol. 8), p. 393.

18) "Answer to Job", *Psychology and Religion* (CW, Vol. 11), p. 460.

19) "On the Nature of the Psyche", *Structure and Dynamics of the Psyche,* pp. 222 f.

20) *Ibid.,* p. 222.

21) J. Goldbrunner, *Holiness is Wholeness, and Other Essays.*

22) "Transformation Symbolism in the Mass", *Psychology and Religion,* pp. 259 f.

23) *Two Essays on Analytical Psychology* (CW, Vol. 7), par. 243, n. 1.

24) "The Meaning of Psychology for Modern Man", *Civilization in Transition* (CW, Vol. 10), p. 140.

25) *Psychology and Alchemy* (CW, Vol. 12), par. 105.

26) *Psychology of the Unconscious,* London, 1917; New York, 1916. (This passage was modified in the revised [1952] edition. Cf. *Symbols of Tranformation* [CW, Vol. 5], p. 417.—Trans.)

27) "The Psychology of the Child Archetype", in *Archetypes and the Collective Unconscious* (CW, Vol. 9, Part I), p. 167.

28) "Psychological Aspects of the Mother Archetype", *ibid.,* pp. 95 f.

The Religious Function
and Conscience

1) Gen. 1:27.

2) J. Rudin, "Psychotherapie und religiöser Glaube", in *Neurose und Religion,* pp. 63 ff.

3) As an example of an "empty" religious attitude Rudin cites the following dream. A patient, who otherwise followed the religious precepts conscientiously, dreamt that she was in a church but was unable to see the sacred action because the whole church was clouded with incense, so that she felt completely disoriented. This was not surprising in view of the "nebulous" situation in which she found herself. (*Op. cit.,* p. 85.)

4) *Psychology and Religion* (CW, Vol. 11), pp. 104 f.

5) "Freud and Jung: Contrasts", in *Freud and Psychoanalysis* (CW, Vol. 4), p. 339.

6) Rudin, *op. cit.,* p. 80.

7) *Ibid.,* p. 88.

8) *Psychology and Alchemy* (CW, Vol. 12), par. 13.

9) Rudin, *op. cit.,* p. 92.

10) *Ibid.,* p. 70.

11) *Ibid.,* p. 93.

12) *Psychology and Alchemy,* par. 15.

13) "The Psychology of the Transference", in *The Practice of Psychotherapy* (CW, Vol. 16), p. 192, n. 44.

14) "A Psychological Approach to the Dogma of the Trinity", *Psychology and Religion* (CW, Vol. 11), pp. 179 f.

15) For a critical confrontation between the views of Freud and Jung, see E. Spengler, *Das Gewissen bei Freud und Jung. Mit einer philosophisch-anthropologischen Grundlegung.*

16) "A Psychological View of Conscience", in *Civilization in Transition* (CW, Vol. 10), p. 454.

17) *Ibid.,* p. 453.

18) *Ibid.,* p. 454.

19) *Ibid.,* pp. 445 f.

20) *Ibid.,* pp. 448 f.

21) Cf. *supra,* p. 51.

22) *Loc. cit.,* p. 447.

23) *Ibid.*, p. 445.

24) *Ibid.*, p. 455.

25) *The Development of Personality* (CW, Vol. 17), pp. 175 f.

26) "Psychotherapists or the Clergy", *Psychology and Religion* (CW, Vol. II), p. 343.

27) This quotation can no longer be located.

The Dual Nature of Man

1) We could conceive of this ethical goal, with Wilhelm Keller, as an inborn "striving for self-value", which constitutes man's human dignity and is a possibility given to him alone. Cf. Keller, *Das Selbstwertstreben*, p. 94.

2) Job 1:6.

3) Victor White, *God and the Unconscious*, pp. 178 ff.

4) *Aion* (CW, Vol. 9, Part III), p. 69 (modified).

5) *Ibid.*

6) *Psychology and Alchemy* (CW, Vol. 12), par. 208. Cf. 2 Cor. 12:7: "And lest I should be exalted above measure through the abundance of the revelations, there was given to me a thorn in the flesh, the messenger of Satan to buffet me".

7) *Memories, Dreams, Reflections*, p. 297 (E. 277).

8) Cf. J. Rudin, "Gott und das Böse bei C. G. Jung", in *Neue Zürcher Zeitung*, 30 July 1961, p. 4.

9) *Aion*, p. 53.

10) Gen. 3:5.

11) *Aion*, p. 267.

12) "And there was evening and morning one day". Gen. 1:5 (Vulgate).

13) "Good and Evil in Analytical Psychology", in *Civilization in Transition* (CW, Vol. 10), pp. 463, 464.

14) "A Psychological Approach to the Dogma of the Trinity", in *Psychology and Religion* (CW, Vol. 11), p. 173 (modified).

15) Cf. in particular *Aion*, ch. V, "Foreword to White's *God and the Unconscious*" (CW, Vol. 11), "Answer to Job" (*ibid.*), and *Mysterium Coniunctionis* (CW, Vol. 14), pp. 544 ff.

16) "Good and Evil in Analytical Psychology", p. 458.

17) "Foreword to White's *God and the Unconscious*", p. 306.

18) Pascal, *Pensées,* pp. 68 and 61.

19) *Ibid.,* p. 60.

20) Exod. 20:13.

21) Hence there are many who keep strictly to the commandment and refuse military service so as not to come into conflict with their own conscience.

22) Exod. 20:12.

23) "Good and Evil in Analytical Psychology", p. 462.

24) While the memoirs were being written (1957 onwards) Jung was still deeply shaken by the evil which assumed unparalleled forms in the Second World War and which we were forced to experience as a reality in our midst.

25) My italics.

26) Jung is really referring here to the admonition of conscience. Cf. *supra,* pp. 114 ff.

27) *Memories, Dreams, Reflections,* pp. 329 f (E. 303–5).

28) W. Keller, *Das Selbstwertstreben,* p. 103: "Self-realization is the deepest desire of being." And p. 76: "For in having to give a shape to himself, the human being has also to be inwardly responsible for himself."

29) *Ibid.,* p. 78: "Neuroses are manifestations of failures in self-realization."

30) The liturgy for Easter Eve speaks, in the Exultet, of the *felix culpa* of our first parents; without it, humanity would not have travelled the road of conscious realization.

31) Vulgate: *"Seipsos castraverunt".*

32) Matt. 19:12.

33) Matt. 5:45, 48.

34) "Analytical Psychology and Weltanschauung", in *The Structure and Dynamics of the Psyche* (Baynes translation), p. 472.

35) *Psychological Types* (CW, Vol. 6), par. 620.

36) *Memories, Dreams, Reflections,* p. 325 (modified) (E. 300).

37) Cf. *supra,* pp. 49 ff.

38) This necessary change into the opposite is inherent in the polaristic nature of the psyche, on which depends its capacity for self-regulation. This regulating function was known already to Heraclitus; he called it *"enantiodromia",* the counterplay of movements. Cf. *Psychological Types,* Definition 18.

39) It is significant that the word "happiness" does not occur once in the Bible.

Conclusion

1) *Symbols of Transformation* (CW, Vol. 5), p. 356.
2) "The Stages of Life", in *The Structure and Dynamics of the Psyche,* p. 394.

BIBLIOGRAPHY

ADLER, G. *Studies in Analytical Psychology*. London and New York, 1948.

APULEIUS. *The Golden Ass*. Translated by Robert Graves. (Penguin Classics), Harmondsworth, 1954.

AVALON, A. *The Serpent Power*. London, 1931.

BACHOFEN, J. *Mutterrecht und Urreligion*. Stuttgart, 1861.

BASH, K. W. "Zur Psychologie akuter symptomatischer Psychosen", in *Der Nervenarzt*, Berlin, 28. Jg., Heft 5, 20 May 1957.

BERTHELOT, M. *Collection des anciens alchimistes grecs*. Paris, 1887–88. 3 vols. See also the new English translation by F. S. Taylor: *Ambix*, I, 1937.

BRAUN, O. *Aus nachgelassenen Schriften eines Frühvollendeten*. Leipzig, 1921.

BRUNNER, C. *Die Anima als Schicksalsproblem des Mannes*. Zurich, 1963.

BÜHLER, Ch. *Der menschliche Lebenslauf als psychologisches Problem*. Leipzig, 1933.
From Birth to Maturity: an Outline of the Psychological Development of the Child. Translated by Esther and William Menaker. London and New York, 1935.

CARUS, C. G. *Psyche*. Stuttgart, 1931 (orig. 1846).
Psychologie. Leipzig, 1808, 2 vols.

CASEL, O. *Das christliche Festmysterium*. Paderborn, 1941.
Das christliche Kultusmysterium. Regensburg, (2nd edn.), 1935.

CUMONT, F. *The Mysteries of Mithra*. Translated from 2nd revised French edn. by T. J. McCormack. London, 1903 (1962); New York, 1957.

DIETERICH, A. *A Mithraic Ritual*. London, 1907.

Nekya. Leipzig, 1913.

ECKHART, MEISTER. *Works*. Translated by C. de B. Evans. London, 1924–52, 2 vols. (Translated from the Pfeiffer edition.)

A Modern Translation. Translated by Raymond B. Blakney. New York, 1941.

EISLER, R. *Handwörterbuch der Philosophie*. Berlin, 1913.

Wörterbuch der philosophischen Begriffe, Vol. I. Berlin, 1910.

ELIADE, M. *Birth and Rebirth*. Translated by W. R. Trask. New York, 1958.

The Myth of the Eternal Return. Translated by W. R. Trask. New York, 1954.

Shamanism: Archaic Techniques of Ecstasy. Translated by W. R. Trask. New York, 1964.

EVANS-WENTZ, W. Y. *The Tibetan Book of the Dead*. With a commentary by C. G. Jung. London and New York, 1957.

FESTUGIÈRE, A. *La révélation d'Hermes Trismégiste*. 3 vols. Paris, 1947.

FIERZ-DAVID, L. *The Dream of Poliphilo*. Translated by Mary Hottinger. London and New York, 1950.

FORDHAM, M. "On the Origins of the Ego in Childhood", in *Studien zur Analytischen Psychologie*, Vol. I. Zurich, 1955.

The Life of Childhood. London, 1944.

FRANZ, M.-L. von. *Kommentar zu "Reich ohne Raum" von Bruno Goetz*. Zurich, 1963.

FRAZER, J. *The Golden Bough*. Abridged edition. London, 1924; New York, 1958.

FREY-ROHN, L. "Die Anfänge der Tiefenpsychologie". Von Mesmer zu Freud. In *Studien zur Analytischen Psychologie*, Vol. I. Zurich, 1955.

FROBENIUS, L. *Das Zeitalter des Sonnengottes*. Berlin, 1904.

GOETHE, J. W. *Faust, Parts One and Two*. Translated by Philip Wayne. (Penguin Classics), Harmondsworth and Baltimore, 1949, 1959.

GOETZ, B. *Reich ohne Raum*. Constance, 1925.

GOLDBRUNNER, J. *Holiness is Wholeness, and Other Essays*. Notre Dame (Indiana), 1964.

GRIMM, W. *Tierfabeln bei den Meistersängern*. Berlin, 1855.

GUNKEL, H. *Schöpfung und Chaos in Urzeit und Endzeit*. Göttingen, 1895.

HARDING, E. *Journey into Self.* An Interpretation of Bunyan's *Pilgrim's Progress.* New York, 1956.

HAUER, J. W. *Seminar Notes on Tantra Yoga.* Privately multigraphed by the Psychology Club, Zurich, 1932.

HENTZE, C. *Tod, Auferstehung und Weltordnung.* Zurich, 1955.

HESIOD. *Works.* Translated by Arthur S. Day. London, 1934.

HESSE, H. *Demian.* Translated by W. J. Strachan. London, Peter Owen, and Vision Press, 1958; New York, 1965.

HOLLANDER, E. *Wunder, Wundergeburt und Wundergestalt.* Stuttgart, 1921.

HOSTIE, R. *Religion and the Psychology of Jung.* Translated by G. R. Lamb. London and New York, 1957.

JACOBI, J. *Complex/Archetype/Symbol in the Psychology of C. G. Jung.* Translated by Ralph Manheim. New York, 1959.

"Das Kind wird ein Ich", in *Heilpädagogische Werkblätter.* Lucerne, 1952.

"Ich und Selbst in der Kinderzeichnung", in *Schweizerische Zeitschrift für Psychologie,* Heft 1. Bern, 1955.

"Jungs Beitrag zur Psychologie des Kindes", in *Der Psychologe,* Heft 10. Bern-Schwarzenburg, 1950.

JAFFÉ, A. "*Der Tod des Vergil* von Hermann Broch", in *Studien zur Analytischen Psychologie,* Vol. II. Zurich, 1955.

JUNG, A. "Buchbesprechung von R. Hostie, *Jung und die Religion*", in *Anima,* Heft 4. Olten, 1957.

JUNG, C. G. "Aims of Psychotherapy", in *The Practice of Psychotherapy,* q.v.

Aion (Collected Works, Vol. 9, Part II). London and New York, 1959.

Alchemical Studies (Collected Works, Vol. 13). London and New York, 1967.

"Analytical Psychology and Education", in *The Development of Personality,* q.v.

"Analytical Psychology and Weltanschauung", in *The Structure and Dynamics of the Psyche,* q.v.

"Answer to Job", in *Psychology and Religion: West and East,* q.v.

The Archetypes and the Collective Unconscious (Collected Works, Vol. 9, Part I). London and New York, 1959.

"Brother Klaus", in *Psychology and Religion: West and East,* q.v.

Civilization in Transition (Collected Works, Vol. 10). London and New York, 1964.

"Commentary on *The Secret of the Golden Flower*", in *Alchemical Studies,* q.v.

"Commentary on *The Tibetan Book of the Dead*", in *Psychology and Religion: West and East,* q.v.

"Concerning Mandala Symbolism", in *The Archetypes and the Collective Unconscious,* q.v.

"Concerning Rebirth", in *The Archetypes and the Collective Unconscious,* q.v.

The Development of Personality (Collected Works, Vol. 17). London and New York, 1954.

Exercitia Spiritualia of St. Ignatius of Loyola. Notes on lectures given at the Eidgenössische Technische Hochschule (Federal Polytechnical Institute), Zurich, June 1939–March 1940. Privately multigraphed.

"Foreword to White's *God and the Unconscious*", in *Psychology and Religion: West and East,* q.v.

"Freud and Jung: Contrasts", in *Freud and Psychoanalysis,* q.v.

Freud and Psychoanalysis (Collected Works, Vol. 4). London and New York, 1961.

"General Aspects of Dream Psychology", in *The Structure and Dynamics of the Psyche,* q.v.

"The Gifted Child", in *The Development of Personality,* q.v.

"Good and Evil in Analytical Psychology", in *Civilization in Transition,* q.v.

"The Meaning of Psychology for Modern Man", in *Civilization in Transition,* q.v.

Memories, Dreams, Reflections. Recorded and edited by Aniela Jaffé. Translated by Richard and Clara Winston. London and New York, 1963.

Mysterium Coniunctionis (Collected Works, Vol. 14). London and New York, 1963.

"On Psychic Energy", in *The Structure and Dynamics of the Psyche,* q.v.

"On the Nature of the Psyche", in *The Structure and Dynamics of the Psyche,* q.v.

"On the Psychology and Pathology of So-called Occult Phenomena", in *Psychiatric Studies,* q.v.

"The Philosophical Tree", in *Alchemical Studies,* q.v.

The Practice of Psychotherapy (Collected Works, Vol. 16). London and New York, 1954; revised edition, 1966.

Psychiatric Studies (Collected Works, Vol. 1). London and New York, 1957.

"A Psychological Approach to the Dogma of the Trinity", in *Psychology and Religion: West and East,* q.v.

Psychological Types. Translated by H. G. Baynes, London and New York, 1923.

"A Psychological View of Conscience", in *Civilization in Transition,* q.v.

Psychology and Alchemy (Collected Works, Vol. 12). London and New York, 1953; revised edition, 1967.

"Psychology and Literature", in *The Spirit in Man, Art, and Literature,* q.v.

Psychology and Religion: West and East (Collected Works, Vol. 11). London and New York, 1958.

"Psychology of the Child Archetype", in *The Archetypes and the Collective Unconscious,* q.v.

"The Psychology of the Transference", in *The Practice of Psychotherapy,* q.v.

The Psychology of the Unconscious. London and New York, 1917 and 1916.

"Psychotherapists or the Clergy", in *Psychology and Religion: West and East,* q.v.

Seelenprobleme der Gegenwart. Zurich, 1931.

"The Soul and Death", in *The Structure and Dynamics of the Psyche,* q.v.

The Spirit in Man, Art, and Literature (Collected Works, Vol. 15). London and New York, 1966.

"The Stages of Life", in *The Structure and Dynamics of the Psyche,* q.v.

The Structure and Dynamics of the Psyche (Collected Works, Vol. 8). London and New York, 1960.

"A Study in the Process of Individuation", in *The Archetypes and the Collective Unconscious,* q.v.

Symbols of Transformation (Collected Works, Vol. 5). London and New York, 1956.

"Synchronicity: An Acausal Connecting Principle", in *The Structure and Dynamics of the Psyche,* q.v.

"The Transcendent Function", in *The Structure and Dynamics of the Psyche*, q.v.

"Transformation Symbolism in the Mass", in *Psychology and Religion: West and East*, q.v.

Two Essays on Analytical Psychology (Collected Works, Vol. 7). London and New York, 1953; revised edition, 1966.

"The Undiscovered Self", in *Civilization in Transition*, q.v.

"Woman in Europe", in *Civilization in Transition*, q.v.

JUNG, C. G., AND KERENYI, C. *An Introduction to a Science of Mythology*. London, 1950. Titled *Essays on a Science of Mythology*, New York, 1949. The latter published as a paperback in Harper Torchbooks, New York, 1963.

JUNG, C. G., AND WILHELM, R. *The Secret of the Golden Flower*, with a Commentary by C. G. Jung. Translated by Cary F. Baynes. Revised edition, London and New York, 1962.

KELLER, W. *Das Selbstwertstreben*. Munich and Basel, 1963.

KERENYI, K. *Die Mysterien von Eleusis*. Zurich, 1962.

"Vater Helios", in *Eranos-Jahrbuch 1943*. Zurich, 1944.

LA ROCHEFOUCAULD, F. *The Moral Maxims and Reflections of the Duke de la Rochefoucauld*. Translated by G. H. Powell. London, 1924.

LENNHOFF, E. *Die Freimaurer*. Vienna, 1932.

LEWIS, E. *Children and Their Religion*. London and New York, 1962.

LOCKE, J. *An Essay Concerning Human Understanding*, ed. John W. Yolton. London, 1961.

NEUMANN, E. *Das Kind*. Zurich, 1963.

The Origins and History of Consciousness. Translated by R. F. C. Hull. New York and London, 1954.

"Die Psyche und die Wandlung der Wirklichkeitsebenen", in *Eranos-Jahrbuch 1951*. Zurich, 1952.

OTTO, R. *The Idea of the Holy*. Translated by J. W. Harvey. Oxford, 1926; New York, 1950. Pelican Books, 1959.

OVID. *The Metamorphoses of Ovid*. Translated and with an introduction by Mary M. Innes. Harmondsworth and Baltimore, 1955.

PASCAL, B. *Pensées*. Translated by John Warrington. London, 1960.

PEUKERT, W. E. *Die Rosenkreuzer*. Jena, 1928.

PLATO. *The Symposion*. Translated by W. Hamilton. Harmondsworth and Baltimore, 1951.

RADIN, P. *World of Primitive Man.* (Evergreen), New York, 1960.

RAHNER, H. "The Christian Mystery and the Pagan Mysteries", in *The Mysteries, Papers from the Eranos Yearbooks,* Vol. 2. Translated by Ralph Manheim. New York and London, 1955.

REITMAN, F. *Psychotic Art.* London, 1950; New York, 1951.

RUDIN, J. "Gott und das Böse bei C. G. Jung", in *Neue Zürcher Zeitung,* 30 July 1961, p. 4.

"Psychotherapie und religiöser Glaube", in *Neurose und Religion.* Olten, 1964.

SAINT-EXUPÉRY, A. *The Little Prince.* Translated by Katherine Woods. London and New York, 1944.

SCHICK, H. *Das ältere Rosenkreuzertum.* Berlin, 1942.

SCHILLER, F. VON. *The Poems of Schiller.* Translated by E. P. Arnold Forster. London, 1901.

SCHMIDT, H. *Philosophisches Wörterbuch.* Stuttgart, 1934.

SPEISER, F. *Ueber Initiationen in Australien und Neuguinea.* Basel, 1942.

SCHOPENHAUER, A. *Essays from the Parerga and Paralipomena.* Translated by T. Bailey Saunders. London, 1951.

SCHWARZ, O. *Sexualität und Persönlichkeit.* Vienna, Leipzig, Bern, 1934.

SIEBENTHAL, W. VON. *Die Wissenschaft vom Traum.* Berlin, 1953.

SMITH, E. *The Evolution of the Dragon.* Manchester, 1919.

SPENGLER, E. *Das Gewissen bei Freud und Jung.* Zurich, dissertation, 1964.

VISCHER, A. L. *Old Age, its Compensations and Rewards.* Translated by B. Miall. London, 1947; New York, 1948.

WHITE, V. *God and the Unconscious.* London, 1952; New York, 1961.

WICKES, F. *The Inner World of Childhood.* New York, 1927.

WOODS, R. *The World of Dreams.* New York, 1947.

WUNDT, W. *Ethik.* Stuttgart, 1886; 5th edn., 1923–24.

ZWINGLI, U. *De vera et falsa religione.* Tiguri (Froschauer), 1525.

The Latin Works of H. Zwingli. Edited by Samuel Macauley Jackson. Philadelphia, 1922–29.

INDEX